I'm a Believer

Micky Dolenz

and Mark Bego

I'm a Believer

My

Life of

Monkees,

Music, and

Madness

Cooper Square Press

Published by Cooper Square Press
An imprint of The Rowman & Littlefield Publishing Group, Inc.
200 Park Avenue South, Suite 1109
New York, New York 10003-1503
www.coopersquarepress.com

Distributed by National Book Network

A previous edition of this book was catalogued as follows by the Library of Congress:

Dolenz, Micky.
    I'm a believer : my life of Monkees, music, and madness / Micky Dolenz and Mark
Bego.—1st ed.
        p. cm.
    Discography: p.
    Includes index.
    1. Dolenz, Micky. 2. Monkees (Musical group) 3. Rock musicians—United
States—Biography. I. Bego, Mark. II. Title.
ML420.D58A3 1993
782.42166'092—dc20
[B]   93-15551

ISBN 978-0-8154-1284-7

Manufactured in the United States of America.
⊖™ The paper used in this publication meets the minimum requirements of American
National Standard for Information Sciences—Permanence of Paper for Printed Library
Materials, ANSI/NISO Z39.48-1992.

This book is dedicated to my mother,
my father, and my children.
The circle is complete.

Acknowledgments

The authors would like to thank the following for their information, inspiration, and contributions in preparing and delivering
this book:

Kevin and Robyn Allyn

Steve Cox

Henry Diltz

Samantha Dolenz

Ami Dolenz

Fed Ex

Jeff Forrester

Ron Goldfarb

Nina Graybill

Stuart Gross

Hennessy X.O.

Randy Johnson

The Mayfield Inn

Maggie McManus

Microsoft Word

Mary Ann Naples

Brookes Nolhgren

Marisa Redanty

Joe Russo

Janelle Scott

Barbara Shelley

Gary Strobel

Contents

Contents

Preface

hen I was originally asked to write this book I must admit I was somewhat reluctant—for a number of reasons.

1. It's too soon to "sum up" my life. I'm only forty-eight.
2. I'm not a fan of show-biz autobiographies.
3. Autobiographies tend to be regarded as obituaries!

I was, however, finally convinced to do it (obviously), but please let me make a few things clear.

First of all, this is not intended as a definitive Monkeeology. Though I have included a discography at the back of the book, there's actually very little factual information regarding Monkee-dates, Monkeesales, Monkeethis, or Monkeethat. This book is about my life to date, including, but not limited to, my experiences vis-à-vis the Monkees.

Secondly, I'm not alleging that the events I describe took place in exactly the way that I describe them, only that it's the way that I remember them happening at the time. (Anyone who has seen or read *Rashomon* will understand what I mean.)

Finally, I don't believe that, on the whole, any of this: rock & roll, pop music, movies, and TV (*especially* TV) is really very important in the grand scheme of things. Don't get me wrong, *art* is important—but so little of what we see and hear can really be described as much more than brain candy. Not that there is anything wrong with candy. It's full of flavor, somewhat nutritious, and relatively harmless. (Just make sure you brush your brain afterwards.) But two hundred years from now I doubt if much of what we consider so important and profound today will even be remembered, much less studied or revered.

Does this sound ungrateful? Here I am, someone who has made a very comfortable living in TV, radio, pop music, etc., casting aspersions. That's not the point. I'm just suggesting that we not take it all too seriously. There's much more to life than listening to and watching others pretending that *they* have a life. After you read this book—maybe have a few laughs, raise your eyebrows a few times—put in on the shelf. Turn off the TV, turn off the CD player, and *do* something, for your family, for your community, for yourself.

MICKY DOLENZ
Los Angeles, California

I'm a Believer

Too Much Monkee Business

> It was the best of times,
>
> it was the worst of times.
>
> —Charles Dickens
> *A Tale of Two Cities*

Fade In:
Ext. Backstage—Universal Amphitheatre—Night

It's September 5, 1986, and the night of the MTV Music Video Awards. THE MONKEES: DAVY JONES, PETER TORK, and MICKY DOLENZ are waiting backstage to go on and present an award. In the wings, Whitney Houston, Janet Jackson, and others are waiting to perform.

Davy Jones is furious. He has been told by Arista Records that the next MONKEE single is going to be "Anytime, Anyplace, Anywhere," a new cut off the *Then & Now . . . The Best of the Monkees* album and a follow-up to their recent Top Twenty record "That Was Then, This Is Now."

When the Arista deal had been made, Davy had chosen not to join Micky and Peter on the recordings and proceeded to go ballistic when "That Was Then, This Is Now" became a hit.

The three aging pop stars are screaming at each other.

DAVY

If Arista releases another song off that album I'll ruin this group!

PETER

Hey, man. Lighten up!

MICKY
(to Davy)

It was your fault for not signing the Arista deal. It was a golden opportunity!

DAVY

They're bloodsucking thugs! They just want to rip us off!

MICKY

Those bloodsucking thugs just got us a hit record, you asshole!

PETER

There's no need for name-calling.

MICKY

Fuck off!

The other celebrities, reporters, and pop personnel gathered backstage can't help but hear what is going on. They cringe with embarrassment and tactfully start to drift away. DAVID FISHOF the sleazy, would-be Monkee producer/manager is attempting to arbitrate.

FISHOF

Come on, guys. It's a big night. We can work this out later.

DAVY

Fuck off!

An assistant stage manager timidly approaches the fuming trio.

ASM
(tentatively)

Excuse me. But you guys are on in one minute.

The three Monkees quickly disperse in separate directions.

Cut to:

Int. Backstage—Universal Amphitheatre—Night

Davy, Micky, and Peter arrive backstage and hover around—waiting to be introduced. They don't speak to each other.

ANNOUNCER

And now to present our next award. The Monkees!

The crowd goes wild. The cameras pan to the wings, and in bounce the Monkees, smiling and strutting, for all appearances the best of friends. They read their corny award-show dialogue, present the award, and with a wave, bounce off stage. They don't speak to each other for a month.

Fade Out

For me, the whole Monkees' saga was one continuous high, right up to the last moments at the end of our incredibly successful reunion in 1986.

Unlike so many acts, whose moment in the sun comes but once, we had the unique opportunity to recapture the fun, magic, and success that had been the trademark of the Monkees since their inception in 1966.

I had gone into the reunion project with high hopes. Having moved to England in the mid-seventies and become a successful producer/director, I was ready to get back on the stage, team up with my old buddies, and relive those "zany" days. Like most groups who experience the kind of heady success that we had enjoyed, we had had our problems, our disagreements, our confrontations. But, as they say, time heals all wounds, and I only remembered the good times, not the bad. I wasn't lugging around any old baggage or harboring any animosities. Unfortunately, there were others in the group who were. When I watched the act disintegrate into a war of petty squabbles and ego battles it not only took me by surprise, it broke my spirit.

I had seen so clearly the potential that this reunion represented—for all of us to share. The concert tour was a box-office smash (it was the top-grossing tour of 1986), we were the darlings of MTV, our new single had gone Gold and our album, Platinum. All of these accomplishments were unheard of for a group that hadn't released a record in twenty years. Offers were coming in from left and right, from movies to TV specials to megabuck commercials. The consensus of the press was, "It's the most amazing comeback in rock & roll history!"

It all started with Arista records coming to us in early 1986 and asking if we wanted to record some new tracks for an album of greatest hits they were planning to release to coincide with our upcoming tour. The tour itself had been prompted by the success of the marathon Monkees reruns on MTV. Naturally, I said yes. Unbelievably, Davy turned them down. And Peter was expressing reservations. Michael Nesmith had been approached about getting involved in the reunion project but had declined due to his commitments at his very successful production company, Pacific Arts.

Arista Records held the rights to the Monkees' recording catalogue, and the trademarked name, so there wasn't any question of being able to record for any other label. It was simply too good an opportunity to pass up. I jumped at the chance and was stunned that anybody would have even a moment's hesitation.

Arista hired a strong producer, Michael Lloyd, to helm the project. They picked some great songs and booked the recording sessions. I didn't want to go ahead without a consensus from Davy and Peter, but we had to record the vocals within a week or else Arista wouldn't be able to get the record out in time to take advantage of the tour. It was coming down to the wire.

Davy held fast. Peter, kind soul that he is, kept vacillating back and forth; trying to decide what to do by meditating and consulting the *I Ching*. Since I had sung most of the leads on the original Monkee records, Arista finally decided that they would go with just my vocals if Davy wouldn't change his mind. He didn't. Finally, I managed to convince Peter to come in and sing on the tracks with me, and we finished the songs within hours of having to leave on tour. I was thrilled, Peter was ambivalent, and Davy was enraged.

He was so upset that he boycotted the record and Arista all together. He wouldn't allow any of the record company executives backstage, refused to do any press or radio interviews associated with the record, refused to be on stage when Peter and I performed the new song, insisted that the music video for the record be restaged and shot *after* a concert, and Peter and I had to accept our Gold Records in the basement of some concert hall, lest Davy see us and throw a tantrum.

I tried time and time again to smooth his ruffled feathers. I negotiated with Arista and they agreed, reluctantly, to let him sign on to the deal after the fact. He wouldn't. He flatly refused, and his wife—who was managing him at the time—also dug her heels in. There was no changing his mind.

Since "That Was Then, This Is Now" had sold so well, Arista wanted to follow it up immediately with another release. They informed Peter and me what their intentions were, and Davy found out through the grapevine. The scene that began this book was the result.

The next day I got a call from Roy Lott at Arista Records who told me, "I can't release another record off the new album or Davy will quit the group. I don't want to be known as the man who broke up the Monkees." He informed me that they were going to rerelease the original Monkee version of "Daydream Believer." They did and it bombed.

To make matters worse, more than worse, MTV had graciously invited the Monkees to play at their prestigious "Superbowl Tailgate Party." David Fishof had accepted on our behalf (albeit without our actual consent), and at the last minute, Davy decided he didn't want to participate. His attitude was simply, "MTV needs us more than we need MTV."

It was around this time that I remember thinking, "This is how it must have felt on board the *Titanic.*" MTV instantly banned us from the air, and Arista Records dropped our contract. Consequently, the 1987 tour didn't generate half of the excitement or the revenues that we had enjoyed in '86.

Shakespeare wrote in *Julius Caesar,* "There comes a tide in the affairs of men, which taken at the flood, leads on to fortune." Well, we not only missed the tide, we set the sails on fire and scuttled the ship.

In all fairness to David, some of the difficulties we faced boiled down to the same problem that had always plagued the Monkees since the cancellation of the TV show way back in 1968. To stick with the seagoing metaphor, we had been left without a captain to guide our ship of fools.

Remember, *The Monkees* was a television show *about* a group and, even though we did become a group in every sense of the word, the initial project included producers, directors, writers, and a host of support personnel. Michael Nesmith once said, "If you want to get the Monkees group back together, you really have to include Bob Rafelson (producer/creator/director); Bert Schneider (producer/creator); Lester Sill and Donnie Kirshner (musical directors); Tommy Boyce and Bobby Hart (record producers/song writers); and Carole King, Neil Diamond, Harry Nilsson, Paul Williams, David Gates, and Carole Bayer Sager to write the songs.

In 1986 we were foolishly trying to do it all by ourselves, and there were some of us who thought we could fill the shoes of all those incredibly talented and powerful people by ourselves. Big Mistake!

For my part, I was trying to create a *new* apparatus to take the place of the original organization that had driven the Monkee machine. I courted several high-powered movers and shakers in the industry; I mediated, debated, argued, lectured, cajoled, guided, cried, and begged. I used everything I had learned as a producer and director to try and keep the project alive, but found I was spending most of my time in damage control. And what was worse, most of my work was met with either suspicion or jealousy.

Being the constant optimist, I did continue to work on various Monkee projects after the Arista and MTV fiascoes. But it was all to no avail: Negotiations would be finalized and then reneged on, our services would be pledged then held as ransom to elicit a better deal, promises would be made then broken, projects started then sabotaged, there were a number of lawsuits filed and more pending. The only ones who loved us more than our fans were our lawyers. It was endless, and heartbreaking.

On July 10, 1989, I suddenly found myself reunited with Davy, Peter, and Mike. The occasion was the presentation of a Monkees star on Hollywood Boulevard's Walk of Fame. We were surrounded by cheering, adoring fans and a battalion of reporters and photographers. I was thrilled and honored by the event.

After the ceremony, the plan was for all of us to get together and discuss the future of the group and the various projects that were being offered or proposed. I thought about it for quite some time. I thought about what the last few years had done to me and my family, about what it had done to my reputation in the industry, about what it had done to my spirit. I didn't show up.

It was time to cut the cord, cut my losses, and put my energies into the one thing I had always believed in—myself.

Two

I Was Born Very Young

The childhood shows the man,

As morning shows the day. Be famous then

By wisdom; as thy empire must extend,

So let extend thy mind o'er all the world.

—John Milton
Paradise Regained

The title of this chapter is an old joke, but sort of appropriate. I was certainly "born" into show business at a very tender age. I was doing screen tests at the age of six.

(I had done some earlier prenatal work, but it's only available on ultrasound.)

My first postnatal work was a screen test for a movie that was to be shot in Mexico. It had the grand title "The Rings Around Saturn."

I was to play a little Mexican boy (with my hair blackened courtesy of the makeup department). At the time, the producers didn't think anything of casting a little American boy to play a little Latino boy, because this was 1951 and the term "politically correct" had not yet been coined. (Nor had "Latino," now that I come to think of it.)

The boy is out in a field one day when a massive meteorite smashes into the ground. Magically, on this meteorite is a bull—a very large enchanted bull that only the little boy can see. The bull of course turns out to be, "dee greydiss bool een awl of Meheeco."

So I did the test, the cast was hired, the locations were picked, and the donuts were bought. Then suddenly, the Mexican population had the audacity to stage a revolt against the then-current oppressive, totalitarian dictatorship of a government, and the project was subsequently shelved.

There's no business like show business.

So the die was cast. As my father was an actor, I suppose it was only natural that I would follow in his footsteps.

His name was George Dolenz and he was born in Trieste, Italy, right on the border of Yugoslavia. Our family name was originally spelled with a t in it: Dolentz. Somewhere along the line the t got dropped. It probably happened when he jumped ship in New York. I suppose there's this t lying around somewhere at the bottom of the Hudson River.

He explained that there was always a war going on in the area, so the borders were constantly changing; hence the name kept changing. It was probably "Dolentzovitch" at one time or the other. (It's nice to see that that region has become so stable.)

He had grown up in a very large family, with lots of brothers, sisters, stepbrothers, stepsisters, etc. They were quite poor and I remembering him telling me how at one time they had nothing to eat but turnips for six months. (I'm not sure if this was entirely true. It was probably said in the spirit of, "I had to crawl naked through the snow for seven miles everyday to go to school.")

The truth is, we know very little about his family, or his past in general. My mother admits that she never went back to Italy to visit his relatives, and he very seldom mentioned his life there. I wasn't kidding about jumping ship in New York. He had been working on the ship as a waiter. So maybe he had come to the States to start a new life and just never looked back.

He landed in the States in the twenties and, along with some buddies, started searching for the streets of gold. Their quest took them to Cuba, Florida, Chicago (where he had to leave quickly because he wouldn't play ball with the mob), Mexico, and finally California.

Along the way he learned English and, in the thirties, acquired citizenship when the American government granted amnesty to many foreign nationals. But until then he was always on the move, working mostly in the restaurant trade (an education that would eventually come in very handy).

Fate and design eventually drew him to Los Angeles and Hollywood. (Lucky for me. I could have grown up as a busboy in Tijuana.)

During the thirties he had worked his way up through the ranks from waiter to maître d', and when he moved to LaLa Land he ended up as head maître d' at the famous and infamous Hollywood hangout called The Trocadero. It was there that he met the famous and infamous Howard Hughes—in the men's room. Howard, in one of his moments of infinite wisdom, signed my father up as a leading man for RKO. He paid my dad lots of money and made him lots of promises, and my father didn't work for six years. (Along with a lot of other stars and starlets who got sucked up into the propwash of Mr. Hughes's ambitions.)

Hughes was famous for signing up talent, yet seldom made any films! He kept my father under contract for five years but only made one film, *Vendetta* (1950). For the most part, Hughes had all of these people on his payroll, *just in case* he suddenly chose to make a film. (In between seducing anything vaguely humanoid and flying wooden airplanes. What a guy!)

Eventually, after his contract with Hughes was up, my dad appeared in a string of movies in the 1950s and early 1960s. These included *My Cousin Rachel* (1952) with Olivia de Havilland; *Wings of the Hawk* (1953) with Van Heflin; *The Last Time I Saw Paris* (1954) with Elizabeth Taylor; *Sign of the Pagan* (1954) with Jeff Chandler; *The Purple Mask* (1955) with Tony Curtis; and *The Four Horsemen of the Apocalypse* (1961) with Glenn Ford.

It was great having an actor as a dad. I often visited the set, hung out with the special effects guys, met the famous stars. The only trouble was, I began to think that *all* fathers were actors. I didn't understand how unique his profession was. He would film only for a few weeks at a time and maybe only once a year; the rest of the time he would be at home. Once my teacher in the third grade asked the class what our fathers did. I said, "He mows the lawn."

He enjoyed moderate success with his film career, and in 1956 landed the starring role in the TV series *The Count of Monte Cristo*. (It was about this sandwich that learns to add.)

Eventually, that successful series generated a certain amount of stardom, and moneydom, and he was able to fulfill his lifelong dream: He bought his own restaurant in Los Angeles, called the Marquis.

My father had always said that he wanted to be an actor, *and* to own his own restaurant, and I'll be damned if that wasn't exactly what he did.

Oh, how I remember that restaurant. The smell of the grease, the roar of the bartenders. (Or was it the smell of the bartenders . . . ?)

Anyway, the restaurant became one of the hottest in L.A., frequented by the movers and shakers of the time: Tony Martin, Frank Sinatra, Van Johnson, John Carradine, Jennifer Jones, Robert Walker, Susan Hayward, Robert Mitchum, Ann Miller, Mickey Rooney, Rossano Brazzi, Mel Ferrer, to name but a few.

To this day I remember the thrill of entertaining all my friends, and especially my girlfriends, at the Marquis. Can you imagine how impressive it must have been to take a date to this throbbing, pulsing hot spot, where José Caricoa was the in-house entertainment, and where she would be serenaded by my father, the "Count of Monte Cristo!" Man, I was in there! Unfortunately, at the age of nine I didn't know where "in there" was, and if I had I wouldn't have know what to do when I got there.

My mother, Janelle Johnson, had been in show business too. Born in 1923 in Austin, Texas, she had packed up her mother and little brother in the family's old Ford coupe and headed out west in the early forties to find fame and fortune in Hollywood. She had been high school valedictorian, a dancer and actress, had won the prestigious Drama Award at the University of Austin, and even had her own local radio show, *Janelle Sings.*

So out she comes to Hollywood to be a star. She's not the type to just hang out in front of Schwabs Drugstore waiting to be discovered, so she trains hard and soon is making films: *Since You Went Away* (1944) with Robert Walker and Jennifer Jones, *The Brute Man* (1946), and performing in plays. In one of the plays, *Return Engagement,* she costars with an up-and-coming actor named George Dolenz.

It must have been love at first curtain call. They married soon after. And in 1945 . . . me.

Unfortunately, after they met, Mom's career took a backseat. These were the days long before fem-lib and, on top of that, my father was *very* Italian. The wife of an Italian man couldn't work! I'm afraid it was always a bone of contention between them, and I fear my mother has always regretted not pursuing her career. It may have been unfortunate for her professional aspirations, but it was very fortunate for her children. My sisters and I had the extreme pleasure of having a real-life mom around all the time, spending all the time . . . with us.

So on March 8, 1945, around 6:30 in the morning, out pops little Micky Dolenz at Cedars of Lebanon Hospital. My proud parents take me home, which at that time consists of a chicken ranch in Tarzana, California. Deep in the San Fernando Valley, (SFV). Very deep.

Eventually, and thanks to ol' Howard, we move to Bing Crosby's former house in Toluca Lake, also in the San Fernando Valley, but not so deep.

It's a huge house and though they had the money to buy it, they really didn't have the money to keep it up. My mother tells the story of a Hollywood tour bus cruising by the house, the driver giving his spiel:

"And this is the house of the famous actor George Dolenz, soon to be seen in the epic motion picture *Vendetta* with Faith Domergue!"

Out in front of the house is a gardener clad in tattered work clothes. He is busily weeding the front lawn. As the bus passes he turns away and hides his face in the shadow of the scruffy old hat he is wearing—it's my father.

When I was three or so we moved from the Bing Crosby house to more moderate accommodations (still in the SFV). This is about the time my neural networks kicked in and booted up my long-term memory.

One of the strongest, and most vivid, of these memories is the weekly test of the local air raid siren.

This was 1950 and the SFV was the home of the Jet Propulsion Lab and Cal Tech and other high-tech-high-security think tanks. They needed to be protected.

So every Friday morning, at 10:00, precisely, this yellow box at the top of a massive wooden telephone pole would wind up and let go with a mind-boggling screech that would rip clean through our Donna Reedborhood for one minute, precisely.

Cut To:

Int. Dolenz House—Day

Little MICKY comes running into the kitchen where MOM is washing and waxing the floor. Micky is terrified. In the BG we can hear the wail of an AIR RAID SIREN.

MICKY

Mommy! Mommy! What's that?

He grabs her and holds on for dear life. Mom keeps working calmly and doesn't even look up.

MOM

Oh, nothing dear. It's just a test warning for *TOTAL ATOMIC WAR!*

Mom's voice soothes the frightened boy and he returns to the backyard where he continues to stockpile mudpies for an up-coming battle with the neighborhood bully.

Fade Out

Mom would eventually go on to explain about the possibility of war with the (shhhh!) Communists!

(You always had to whisper when you said the word "Communists." In fact, to this day I have trouble saying the word in full voice. In fact, I had to have someone else type this paragraph.)

We were also having air-raid drills at school. We would get under our desks and put our arms up over our heads. As if that would have helped. The reality was that if, God forbid, an A-bomb *had* gone off anywhere within a fifty mile radius, and by some miracle my classroom had managed to escape being vaporized, you would have seen, burned into one of the walls, this cute little silhouette of me hiding under my desk—with my arms over my head. The original Crispy Critter.

If you stop to think about it, those were pretty horrific times in which to grow up, but I suppose you can get used to just about anything. On the whole, I remember those early childhood years as happy, content, and normal. I just hung out, and played. Even back then I had interests in mechanics, engineering, science, and especially in science fiction. When I was eight I even tried to build a real airplane out of wood (I must have wanted to keep up with Howard). My best friend at the time was a boy named Chris Evans, and his father had been in the air force. Naturally, I assumed that Chris would *certainly* know how to build an airplane. I turned to him for technical advice. I built it out of two-by-fours and was going to launch it with an inner-tube. I was so disappointed when it wouldn't fly.

I've always had this fascination with flying, even as a child. I used to think about being Superman, and I fantasized about jumping off of the roof with umbrellas as parachutes. Fortunately good sense prevailed and I didn't actually try it. Not until many years later when I took up hang gliding!

I was not an only child growing up. I have three younger sisters. The oldest of the three is "Coco." Her real name is Gemma Marie, but somewhere along the line I nicknamed her "Coco Sunshine" and it stuck. I don't think she has ever forgiven me.

Coco and I were the best of friends for the longest time. Though we often fought like cats and dogs, we had the greatest of times—and the worst of times. We took the term "sibling rivalry" to new dimensions. I suppose she doesn't remember anything but being harassed by her older brother. But what I remember is having a loyal and loving sidekick.

And the clubs! Boy, did we have clubs. A pet club, a bicycle club, a bug club . . . we even had a club that just thought up other clubs.

The best club by far was the Blackhawks. It was based on a famous comic book of the same name about a bunch of superheros zooming about in jet planes yelling "Blaackhaawks!" and saving the world. Coco and I would go zooming around the local streets on our bicycles screaming, "Blaaackhaaawks!" and saving the neighborhood. (The whole world being slightly outside of our purview.) We would be on our own imaginary mission to save the 'hood from all sorts of evil. In those days, most of the local evil was all incarnate within this one kid who lived down the block. His name was Edgar, or something equally as geeky. He was our arch enemy.

I'll never forget one particular episode:

Ripple Dissolve To:

Ext. Dolenz Yard—Day

Micky and *Coco* are standing face to face with *Edgar* and his *henchman*. Edgar has crossed through the neutral zone and is mounting an attack on Federation territory, (i.e., Micky and Coco's driveway). Edgar and Micky hold long bamboo poles as swords. Edgar is bigger than Micky and is slowly getting the upper hand.

MICKY

You dope. Get outta my yard!

EDGAR

Make me!

Edgar takes a swing with his bamboo sword of death. Micky backs up the driveway trying to dodge the deadly attack. Suddenly, unbeknownst to the two combatants, Coco slips around Edgar's flank and in one deft move grabs the bamboo pole out of his hands just as he has raised it over his head to deal the final blow.

Edgar and his henchman are routed. Micky grabs Coco and gives her a huge hug.

MICKY

Coco! You saved me!

Cut To:

Int. Dolenz House—Day

Coco is beaming with pride as Micky pins a "medal" on her chest. The medal is made of aluminium foil and cardboard but it might as well be solid gold.

The music *swells*, (composed by John Williams), and the rebel forces are once again safe from the scourge of the Evil Empire.

Fade Out

Unfortunately, our experiences didn't always end up on such a gallant note. As my little sister, Coco tried desperately to keep up with me—HER BIG BROTHER—but often I was too thoughtless to realize that little girls can't always keep up with big brothers, so I frequently, albeit unintentionally, got her into danger or trouble.

The problem was, my mom and dad had very different ideas about how to raise kids, and this invariably led to confusion about discipline. My mother used reason, and sometimes a spanking; my father used spanking, and sometimes reason.

They often differed on the way to handle a situation; like the time it was decided that I had to have my tonsils out. I was six or seven at the time. My mother recalls wanting to sit me down and say, "Let me tell you what is going to go on in the hospital." My father, on the other hand, said, "Absolutely not! He's just a child. We'll just take him down there and have the tonsils out and be done with it. By the time he comes to, it'll be over."

So they came to me and said, "We're going on a vacation. Put your pajamas on because we're going in the car and you'll sleep while we drive."

The next thing I know we're at the hospital and I'm having an ether mask shoved over my face!

My father was a lovely man but he had some strange ideas about bringing up children. I suppose that where he came from they performed tonsillectomies at home with a pair of scissors and a kitchen knife!

My poor dad just couldn't seem to get it right. When I was eight years old, I decided I wanted to take piano lessons. Every day when I would come home from school, I was supposed to practice. When I didn't, I got spanked! To this day, I can't sit down on a piano bench without my butt hurting. I'm sure that's why I chose guitar over keyboards. It's Pavlovian.

All in all, however, I think I had a pretty normal childhood: baseball, TV, beating up on my little sister. Everything was going along swell until one day I came home from school and told my mother that my leg was hurting. Well, the first thing they thought, of course, was polio! In those days polio was a very serious problem. As it turned out it wasn't polio—thank God. It was a degenerative bone condition called Perthese disease. It was affecting my right hip; the pain was excruciating.

They took me to a doctor and he diagnosed it immediately. The treatment was simple: Don't walk for a year! Try telling that to a otherwise healthy seven-year-old boy.

So for a year I had my right leg slung up behind me in a strap, and I got around on crutches. I don't remember too much about this time in my life. I've probably blocked it out for obvious reasons. I suppose I could spend a couple of thousand dollars in therapy working it out but . . . who cares?

As it turned out I escaped with minor aftereffects. In fact the doctor admitted that I had had an almost miraculous recovery. As it is, I rarely have a problem with the leg unless I stay up too late and don't get enough rest (like in writing this book).

At the time I was diagnosed, I was attending a marvelous private school in the valley: the Eunice Knight Saunders School. It had horseback riding, swimming, archery, art, pottery—in addition to a high level of academics. In fact, Esther Williams, the movie star, used to teach swimming and diving at the school. It was a wonderful institution but is long since gone—having been replaced by a Sunkist office building. I suppose that's better than a minimall.

The good news out of the Perthese disease was that the doctor assured my parents that I would never have to go into the service. My right leg had ended up about one-quarter of an inch shorter than my left one. I would be automatically 4F.

At one point in my life, I was very disappointed by this turn of events. I desperately wanted to be in the marines! I dreamed about going to officer's candidate school and, though it's hard to imagine now, I was really quite gung-ho. As a teenager I even went to a marine camp called the "Devil Pups." My parents decided that it would be good for me to attend for "disciplinary" reasons. It was a kind of boot camp for kids. And they didn't pull any punches. They really showed you what it would be like to be a marine. Well it worked. I never again wanted to be a marine after that.

Fifteen years later, when I was being drafted, I thought the leg problem would get me out of the service. Boy, was I in for a surprise. But more of that later.

Yes, my mom was a real mom's mom. Three square meals a day, whether you wanted them or not. Floors so clean you could eat off them. I used to get up at night to pee and she would make the bed. She was the kind of mother who every Easter would hand-paint every egg. I don't mean just dunk them in food coloring. I mean *paint.* And every Christmas she would paint the Nativity scene on the living room picture window; and every birthday she would turn the house into a kids' fantasyland; and every Halloween the whole house would stink from singed pumpkin flesh. It was great!

Halloween was especially fun because, believe it or not, in those days you could actually walk around the neighborhood in costume and not have to worry about being shot, mugged, raped, or poisoned. I remember the year that someone put chocolate Ex-Lax in a kid's candy bag, and another kid was slashed in the mouth by a razor blade hidden in an apple. That was the night Halloween died.

I seem to remember that my only great disappointment was when I had a birthday party and asked my parents to invite Annette Funicello . . . and she didn't show up. I was devastated. Boy did I have a crush on her. It must have been the big ears . . .

My mother tells me that I was somewhat of an aggressive kid growing up. I guess I had quite a bad temper. The problem was, if I lost it I would pick up the nearest thing to use as a weapon. God forbid it was an ax!

But somewhere along the line they must have tempered my temper because now I only take out my wrath on inanimate objects. Never people. But after all, these objects mustn't be allowed to interfere with our lives, right? I mean, if a telephone is foolish enough to misdial a number for you when you're in a hurry, then the obvious thing to do is to go and get a machete out of your workshop and calmly, but firmly, hack it to pieces, right? We must keep these objects in their places. Don't you agree? I mean, if you open your car door to get out, and it doesn't stay open but rather swings back on your leg, then you must simply get out of the car, grab the door with both hands, and calmly, but firmly, rip it off the hinges. Believe me, this is the only way in which these things will respect you. If you give them an inch they will take a mile.

I suppose this rather disturbing aspect of my personality came from years of not being able to vent my anger on the source of my frustrations. From a very early age I was restricted in my ability to express emotion freely. When you are a "star" and in the public eye, conventional wisdom dictates that you can't simply tell someone who is harassing you to go "Fuck off!" You have to be diplomatic and keep your poise. Think of the bad press! Well I'm not so sure that this is such a great idea. I think if I had been allowed to let go and vent my spleen once in a while, there might be a few more telephones and car doors around today.

Anyway, I'm a great believer in genetics. I'm convinced that a great deal of who and what we are is hard-wired into our genes. I know this is a controversial subject, and has been since Darwin stumbled around the Galápagos Islands sketching birds' beaks, but I for one have no doubts. Let's face it, my father was Italian, my mother Indian and Irish . . . no wonder I have a temper. Just don't get me drunk and pissed off.

So the year is 1955. I'm ten years old—basically your well adjusted, hyperactive, boy's boy. (It's too bad for my mom that they didn't know about white bread and refined sugar back then.)

Here I am surrounded by a loving, if somewhat unconventional, family that includes a doting grandmother, "Mamoo"

(God knows where *that* name came from); a lovable, wayward James-Dean-wannabe uncle named Jack; and various and sundry dogs, cats, lizards, birds, fish, horned toads, rabbits, and every April a bright little yellow Easter chick that Coco and I would lovingly cherish and care for until it no longer amused us. Then, when it eventually died, we would give it a loving and cherished funeral out in the backyard, where we would bury it in a shallow grave, resplendent with a tiny wooden cross made out of Popsicle sticks, and it would lie there in peace for about ten minutes until it was ripped out of the ground by the various and sundry dogs, cats, lizards, birds, and horned toads. Ahhh! Those were the days.

These salad days were proceeding along very nicely when, one day, my mother came to me and said, "Your father's agent has asked if you want to go on an interview for a TV series."

"No," I said firmly. "I have a baseball game I want to go to."

"All right, honey," replied my mom as she went off to apply another coat of wax to the carpet. (Thankfully, my mom wasn't the pushy stage-mother type. There were no cliché commands for me to display "eyes and teeth" in *our* house.)

But the baseball game kind of fell apart because Chris, (remember him?) had been grounded for performing some bizarre experiment on the family cat, so I decided to go to the interview after all. The interview was for the TV series *Circus Boy*. And that decision, that day, changed everything. For better, or for worse, my life was never to be quite the same.

Three

"Lions and Tigers and Bears— Oh My!"

I think I could turn and live with the animals,

they are so placid

and self-contain'd.

—Walt Whitman
Song of Myself

I had been on other interviews before the one for *Circus Boy*. There were a number of adventure shows around at the time, such as *Fury* and *My Friend Flicka* and *The Adventures of Rin Tin Tin*. I had been up for all of them. I was even up for *Lassie,* but they cast a collie instead. I was very disappointed.

The interview itself was held in the heart of Hollywood at Columbia Pictures, in Frank Capra's old office. As a matter of fact, the office wasn't far from the one where I had a similar interview for *The Monkees* show some ten years later! What a coinkeydink.

The interview was fairly typical as interviews go. I walked into a drab, sparsely furnished office and was introduced to a drab, balding casting director who asked me some drab, boring questions about my hobbies and my experience in the business.

He gave me a few scenes from a script I took back into the lobby and rehearsed with my mom; then I did a "cold reading" in front of the producers. They smiled, I smiled, and I said good-bye.

That was it. I didn't think about it again until some weeks later when my parents informed me that I had a call-back for a screen test! Well this was certainly getting interesting. I had already done a screen test for a movie, remember, so I got rather excited and prayed that the government wouldn't fall before *this* show was made.

The screen test went well. I spent a whole day doing different scenes with different actors. Crying scenes, laughing scenes, and "Look out! The lion has escaped!" scenes. Then I took off my makeup, went home, and proceeded to accidently set my sister's hair on fire.

One evening, a few weeks later, my parents took me out to the Marquis for dinner. I don't remember what the pretense was, but I went along. When I got there I noticed that Norman Blackburn, one of the producers of the series was there. Unbeknownst to me, *Circus Boy* had been sold to NBC and *I* had been chosen to play the part of Corky, the Circus Boy!

Sometime toward the end of the meal, the waiters brought out a big cake, complete with candles and decorated with a candy big-top tent. Mr. Blackburn pulled out a hand-drawn scroll, adorned with little cartoon elephants. It read something like this:

And let it be known that

MICKY DOLENZ
shall from this day forth
be known as the one and only
CIRCUS BOY!

Well, I was no fool. I'd been around. Even at the tender age of ten I was well aware of what starring in your own television series could mean. Just think of all the baseball gloves I could buy. Why, I'd be knee-deep in Popsicles! After the congratulations and the celebratory toasts, I excused myself and walked out into the parking lot.

Cut To:

Ext. Marquis Parking Lot—Night

The sights and sounds of world famous Sunset Boulevard glow and throb in the distance. Ten-year-old MICKY comes out of the smoke-filled restaurant to get a breath of fresh air.

Actually, he has left the celebrations to be on his own. He wants to savor the moment. He leans up against a pearl white 1955 gull-wing Mercedes 300SL and looks up at the stars, watching them as they try to twinkle through this new stuff they call smog.

A big grin breaks across his face. A triumphant, delighted, and slightly smug grin.

> **MICKY**
> (à la Macaulay Culkin)

YES!

Fade Out

Of course, Macaulay Culkin hadn't been born yet. In fact his parents probably hadn't been, either, but you get the point.

Not long after that I started working on the preproduction

for the show. First came the wardrobe fittings, the photo shoots, the interviews, more wardrobe fittings, then the makeup tests, more photos, more interviews, more wardrobe fittings, and then they broke the news to me that they were going to bleach my brown hair blond!

Needless to say, I was not too crazy about this idea. And what was worse, I had to go to the *hairdressing* department to get it done. Yuck! Only *girls* went to a hairdresser! They sat me down in a barber's chair, put an apron over my head, and started combing hydrogen peroxide into my scalp—and then pinned it back with *curlers!* I was mortified.

It was also told at this time that the powers-that-be decided to give me a stage name. Originally they wanted it to be Rock Hudson, but that was already taken so they settled on Micky Braddock. (Braddock was a name they'd dredged up from my mother's side of the family. It seems that somewhere in the dim and distant past I am related to one General Braddock who lost some famous battle in some famous war.)

The reasons the producers gave for changing my name were strange, if not inane. First of all, they said, my father was already well known as the Count of Monte Cristo, and they figured that the television viewing audience might get confused. And, second of all, they thought Braddock was just more "American" than Dolenz.

Whatever the reasons, Micky Braddock I became. A blond Micky Braddock. (Did they think blond hair was more American than brown?)

Finally, came the first day of production, and the first scene we were to shoot was the circus parade sequence that opened the show. It was quite spectacular. There were real circus wagons and real acrobats, a brass band, jugglers, clowns, dancing girls, bears, horses, lions (in cages), and elephants. And on top of one particular elephant was . . . right, yours truly. Talk about culture shock. Only the day before I had been playing with Coco, riding my Schwinn Racer down the sidewalk, screaming

"Blaakhaawk" and today I was riding a smelly elephant down a Western movie street, smiling bravely for the cameras but thinking, "Mom! Get me off of this thing!"

My mom, who was always there as my chaperone, was standing off behind the camera, worried sick, but being assured by some assistant director that "everything was just fine." The assistant director was probably thinking, "If she only knew." The elephant was probably thinking, "Yesterday I was minding my own business, stuffing my face with alfalfa, and today I've got some skinny blond kid bouncing around on my back. What a way to make a living."

Unfortunately, the beginning of *Circus Boy* kind of marked the end of my relationship with Coco as pals. I've always regretted that. It wasn't anybody's fault; it was simply a problem without a solution. I would go to work at six or seven in the morning and not return until five or six at night. Then I would have dinner, study my lines, and go to bed to be ready to get up and start all over again the next day. This went on for three years, and I'm afraid Coco got the short end of the deal. My father was off in England shooting his series, my mom was on the set with me (she had to be there by law), so Coco stayed at home with Mamoo. Thank goodness Mamoo was such a caring and conscientious grandmother.

At the end of the three years, Coco and I were very nearly strangers. My parents had certainly done the best they could under the circumstances, but events overtook intentions. It was just the draw of the cards, but it was a shame.

Briefly, *Circus Boy* was a half-hour adventure show about this kid, Corky, who lives with a traveling circus at the turn of the century (the *last* century). His parents, The Flying Falcons, have been killed in a trapeze accident, and he is unofficially adopted by the circus clown, Joey, played by the marvelous actor Noah Beery, Jr. (the nephew of Wallace Beery). Uncle Joey and the rest of the circus characters become my surrogate family and I become the circus mascot. My circus job is to look after the newborn baby elephant, Bimbo. Bimbo becomes my pet, best friend, confidant, and partner in mischievousness. We are inseparable. (Actually, elephants do make great pets, except when they drool or try to jump up in your lap. It's also important to follow them around with a *very large* wheelbarrow and a shovel.)

Working on the show was an invaluable experience and a marvelous adventure. I was constantly surrounded by extremely talented people. Besides Noah Beery, Jr., there was Robert Lowery as Big Tim Champion, the owner of the circus; Guinn Williams as Big Boy; Andy Clyde as Circus Jack; Billy Barty as Little Tom; and guest stars like Charles Bronson and Sterling Holloway.

And the best part of it all was that it was just like living in a real circus. Instead of having to build all the props and sets, the producers had bought an old, out-of-work circus complete with tents, wagons, sideshows, and a midway. And they always hired real circus acts as performers. Over the years I learned how to walk a tightrope, juggle, swing on a trapeze, and stand up on the back of a running horse. Not only did I ride Bimbo the elephant—I rode Brahman bulls, hippos, a rhinoceros, camels, ostriches, bears, and a lion! The lion, called Nuba, was very famous in his own right, being the third generation lion that you see at the beginning of MGM movies. (Would I like to be getting *his* residual checks!)

The show was originally filmed at a place called Corriganville, deep in the San Fernando Valley (very, very deep), named after a famous cowboy star named Crash Corrigan. I drove by there recently and it has been replaced by a Six Flags amusement park. Then, after a massive windstorm trashed the big top tent, we moved into town across the street from the Columbia Ranch in Burbank. I drove by there recently and the lot where we filmed *Circus Boy* has been replaced by a minimall.

The show was in production for three years, and they were heady days indeed. As the star, I was naturally in nearly every scene and usually the focus of the story. The stories were simple but effective, the plots usually revolving around some problem the circus was having with either people, animals, weather, fire, or some other disaster, natural or contrived. Then, toward the end of the show, when everything looked utterly hopeless, Corky and Bimbo would invariably save the day. Like I said, simple but effective.

And what fun! I was always in the action: riding my elephant, or some other exotic beast, racing along in an open buckboard, running through fire and smoke, rain and snow (plastic snow), swimming in lakes, climbing mountains, dodging cattle stampedes, fighting bad guys, falling in love with pretty little turn-of-the-century girls in pretty little turn-of-the-century dresses, training wild animals, learning to be a clown, crying, laughing, yelling, running, jumping out of moving wagons, shooting guns, throwing knives, riding in balloons . . . (and all that was just on the first day of shooting).

Believe it or not, through all that, I only got hurt once, when I was bitten on the hand by an irate chimpanzee who was hungry and thought my finger was a banana.

There was the time, though, when one of the lions got out of its cage and started wandering around the set. I didn't realize it then, but it could have been very serious. That was the first time I'd ever seen my mother lose it. The wranglers were trying to assure her that the big cat was tame, but she wasn't buying it. "Get Micky the f . . . out of there!" she screamed. They did. Quickly.

When I wasn't shooting, I was going to school on the set, and I loved that too. The law requires that children have three hours of school per day, and I welcomed it. It was the only time I got a chance to rest. I had a wonderful private tutor and, consequently, I did very well. By the end of the series, I had skipped ahead two grades. At the time it didn't seem to matter, but it did cause some problems in years to come (more about that later).

Besides filming the show, there were lots of ancillary activities and adventures: The show was very successful so, at one point, someone must have suggested that I do a personal appearance tour. But what could I do? . . . "Hey, that's it! He'll play the guitar, sing a few songs, and Bimbo the elephant will do a few tricks!" So I learned to play the guitar (quickly) and learned a few songs (quickly) and Bimbo the elephant learned a few tricks (quickly) and they packed us up onto a train and off we went around the good old U.S. of A.

Our first "concert date" was at Kennywood Park in Pittsburgh. I'll never forget it because that was where I had my first encounter with "hordes of screaming fans." As you can imagine, it was quite a shock. But it certainly steeled me for my upcoming experience with the Monkees.

In keeping with our TV show, our stage act was very simple but effective. I would come out on stage and sing a few songs with a band. At that time my repertoire consisted of the theme song from the *Circus Boy* TV show and a couple of contemporary hits like "Purple People Eater," and "Witch Doctor." Then I would call for Bimbo and he would come trundling across the stage (being prodded by his handler who stayed a discreet distance away), and I would feed him some peanuts (the elephant, not the handler), and he would slobber all over my hand and I would pretend to put him through his paces. The lumbering animal would dance and turn, wobble and spin, stand on one leg then the other, then I would feed him some more peanuts and he would slobber all over my hand again, and then for the finale, he would rear up on his hind legs, the drums would roll, and I would stand underneath him, strike a dramatic pose, and smile. The crowd would go, "Ohhhh," applaud, and I would bounce off the stage followed by Bimbo, the Slobbering Elephant.

And then there were the parades. For some reason, people must have loved to see this little blond kid riding his elephant down their local main street, because I rode good ol' Bimbo down more streets, behind more high-school bands, (and in front of more wheelbarrows) than I care to remember, including, I might add, Macy's Thanksgiving Day Parade and the Santa Claus Lane Parade in Hollywood.

Now, don't get me wrong, riding an elephant is great fun. But it can have its drawbacks. If you've ever seen elephant's hair, it's as thick as a pencil lead, so when it gets long it can get rather uncomfortable, not unlike sitting on a bed of nails, I imagine. Well, one day I jumped up on Bimbo's back and had a very unpleasant surprise. I complained to Bimbo's handler, Arkey Arkansas (believe it or not that was the name of Bimbo's trainer), and got the shock of my life. Arkey immediately got out a blow torch and proceeded to burn the hair off the creature's back! (Before you jump up and form a Society for the Protection of Hairy Elephants, let me assure you that this procedure is quite safe and doesn't hurt the elephant at all. An elephant's epidermis [the skin's impermeable outer layer] is about half an inch thick, and that's just the dead stuff. To him it probably felt like a hair dryer.)

That first tour was quite an experience. I was given the keys to half a dozen major cities, I held press conferences, did TV talk shows, performed at Radio City Music Hall, rode in limos, and stayed at fancy hotels. I know exactly how Macaulay Culkin must feel (though he probably spends more money in one week on Nikes then I made in a year).

And, believe it or not, I didn't get too spoiled. (Well, there *was* this one time when I was staying at the Waldorf Astoria and I sent back a chocolate éclair because it was filled with whipped cream instead of custard. But, hey . . . whipped cream in an éclair?)

But it wasn't all peaches and whipped cream. It soon became apparent, even to my tiny ten-year-old mind, that not only had I been given a fabulous opportunity but, as the star of a successful TV series, much of the responsibility for that series was resting squarely on my tiny ten-year-old shoulders.

No longer could I wake up in the morning, feign a stomachache, and dodge going to school. No longer could I throw a childish fit because I couldn't get my way. Suddenly I was lifted out of a, more or less, normal existence and dropped into a very unusual, exotic, fairytale world of make-believe, where I existed neither as a child nor an adult but rather in some sort of netherland between.

I was sheltered, yet accountable. Pampered, yet labored. Loved, yet handled with kid gloves (lest I throw a tantrum and have someone fired). For three years I hardly ever met or played with another kid my age. I was surrounded by adults but not treated as one. (The people on the set were not even allowed to curse in front of me.)

It was never said in so many words, but I knew that the other actors, the crew, the producers, NBC, Screen Gems, and the sponsors were all relying on me. Quite a burden. And there was always the threat of "my reputation." Whenever I did start to get out of line, someone would invariably warn me about getting a reputation like Lee Aaker. He was the kid star of *The Adventures of Rin Tin Tin,* and my producers told me that he was known for being difficult to work with and a brat. This confused me because I knew Lee; we used to hang out around the lot. He seemed a pretty nice kid to me. In later years it suddenly occurred to me that his producers were probably saying the same things to him about me!

Funnily enough, there are some striking similarities between the life of a child star and the life of a caged animal. Both are cared for but not allowed to wander too far. Both are nurtured and cosseted but also protected and restrained. And it's a fact that animals in a zoo often take to neurotic and, sometimes, self-destructive behavior. The same could be said of many child stars (and some adults I might add).

It's also a fact that many circus and zoo animals eventually go crazy and have to be destroyed. Unfortunately, this is what happened to Bimbo. One day I was told that I would be getting another baby elephant on the show. I asked why, and my mother explained that Bimbo had turned on Arkey and had been put to sleep. It seems that male elephants in captivity eventually go crazy and have to be destroyed. The same thing sometimes applies to chimpanzees and other wild animals kept in captivity. Needless to say, I was very upset when I heard about Bimbo. Who would slobber on me now?

But, all in all, it was an exciting, fun-filled, unusual, intense period of my life, filled with wonderful people and exciting escapades. Certainly a very strange situation to find myself in at the end of my first decade of life, and it is a great credit to my parents that I came out of the experience as well as I did. At least they didn't have to put *me* to sleep.

Four

Kid on a Hot Convertible Roof

Listen to them—

the children of the night.

What music they make!

—Bram Stoker
Dracula

ne day in 1958 the inevitable happened, *Circus Boy* was cancelled. My parents told me that the producers had said I was growing up too fast and changing from a cute little kid into a gawky teenager, and they couldn't *think* of replacing me. (I think they were just being polite.) Whatever the case, I was out of a job. And, strangely enough, it didn't bother me in the slightest.

I stayed on the Columbia lot for a while, finishing up my school year. That helped to wean me slowly. But basically, I was once again a civilian. (But not just good ol' Micky Dolenz anymore. *Now* it was Micky Dolenz, ECS . . . ex–child star. The type had been cast. And that wouldn't be the last time.)

My parents decided to send me to a child psychiatrist. I was told that he was an "educational counselor" but the truth was, he was a kiddie shrink. They wanted to find out where I was at, i.e., my emotional and intellectual levels. It was one of the smartest things they ever did.

Cut To:

Int. Dr. Kiddieshrink's Office—Day

Outside we hear the quiet hum of traffic on Ventura Boulevard, a street that Tom Petty will one day make famous in his song "Into the Great Wide Open."

Micky is wandering around a small office while Dr. Kiddieshrink is watching him intently. The doctor speaks quietly and deliberately with a heavy German accent. (Actually, he wasn't German at all, but it will help with the dramatic effect.)

DR. KIDDIESHRINK

Zo. How do you feel about your elephant?

MICKY

He's dead now.

DR. KIDDIESHRINK

Does zat disturb you?

MICKY

No. He slobbered.

Dr. Kiddieshrink opens up a folder of Rorschach ink blots and shows one to Micky.

DR. KIDDIESHRINK

Tell me, Micky. Vaht do you zink zees picture iz?

Micky studies the image for a couple of moments.

MICKY
(*confidently*)

It's a black hawk, holding a key to a city, being squashed by a giant elephant turd.

The doctor's eyes widen, he quickly shuts the folder, and reaches for the phone. Micky starts to circle the room humming "Purple People Eater."

Fade Out

This may be slightly exaggerated, but not much. I was probably pretty screwed up. Who wouldn't be? At any rate, after my parents got the psychiatrist's report they made another very important decision. They took me out of show business altogether. Immediately.

Years later, they told me that I had been offered another series by the same producers called *Cabin Boy* (presumably about a kid on a sailing ship), but they had turned it down. That was the second smartest thing they ever did.

The tragic stories of burned out, drugged out, suicidal ex–child stars are numerous. I've thought about this a lot over the years, and I'm sure that it's the decline and fall of child stars that causes the greatest damage, not the success. Success is fairly easy to handle, for anybody. You may get an inflated ego and turn into an asshole, but that's not nearly as bad as the rejection you experience once you have been on top and suddenly find yourself on the bottom. Let's face it, that's not easy for an adult, much less a child. At least an adult has had some years of experience, in school and in life, to learn to cope with losing, with rejection. A child has little to draw from. One day you're the flavor of the month and the next day you can't get a bit part on *Gunsmoke*. And you don't know why . . . "Don't they like me anymore?"

Many times the parents actually become part of the problem rather than part of the solution. They get as infatuated with the lifestyle of their rich and famous kid as everyone else. One particular ECS I met up with recently told me that his ex-wife lives in one of his expensive homes, his mother in another. He lives in a trailer. My parents saved me from this fate. I quit on top.

So one day I'm riding my elephant down Fifth Avenue in New York City, and the next day I'm riding my bicycle to junior high school in North Hollywood, California. And I couldn't have been happier. I was back on the streets and back to being just one of the kids . . . well, almost.

The first day at school I found myself backed up against a wall, surrounded by a horde of curious students who wanted to take a look at the token celebrity. I never felt so self-conscious in my life. Here I was just trying to fit in; no costume, no elephant, no makeup. But they wouldn't let me alone. And to make matters worse, my blond hair was growing out and the roots were showing! How humiliating. I think I'm still overly self-conscious to this day because of that incident. In fact, when

I'm at a football game, and they're in the huddle, I think they're talking about me.

But all in all the transition back to civilian life was pretty smooth. I made some friends and did very well academically. Too well, it seems. Since I'd skipped a couple of grades during the *Circus Boy* years, I found my classwork easy and sometimes boring. And what was worse, I was nearly two years younger than most of my classmates. Back to Dr. Kiddieshrink.

This time he recommends that I take the ninth grade over again. After I had already graduated! That way I would be among kids my own age and be more likely to adjust socially.

So off I went to another junior high school, another set of friends, and another set of classes, taking the very same subjects that I had just completed. In retrospect this was probably not such a good idea. Though it accomplished the goal of balancing my social scales, I soon became very bored with school in general and never quite got my enthusiasm back.

It was also kind of tough to get too excited about the provincial activities. After flying around the world, staying at the Waldorf, and being the object of affection of thousands of adoring fans, it was difficult to get very excited about the local football game. I regret this. I feel that I missed a part of my life that I can never regain. It is during these school years that one learns social skills and develops his or her mechanisms for creating and dealing with relationships. I missed out on a lot of this. (There are definitely a few pages on relationships missing from my instruction manual.)

While I was struggling with my new role as commoner, my family was growing fast. Two new additions had arrived between the end of *Circus Boy* and the beginning of my high school career. Two lovely little girls named Deborah and Gina. Hurray! More sisters to beat up on! This must have been a real strain on my mom and dad, though. Coco and I had all but made it through the first stage of our respective childhoods (I was fourteen and Coco was ten), when along comes another whole family. But good old Mom and Dad took it in stride, and soon the house was once again festooned with hand-painted Easter eggs and reeking of charred pumpkins.

Meanwhile, I'm at school, adapting to my new role as token celebrity and school mascot. I'm still quite young for my class and even younger for my age, so I'm regarded as "cute" by the bitchin' girls, and a "wimp" by the macho-hunk-jock-dudes. And every semester there's this one new kid in town who has to make a name for himself by punching me in the mouth. It got to the point where I could spot them coming and would punch myself in the mouth to save them the trouble.

But I eventually settle in, make a new best friend, Ricky Gelb, and together we start doing all the *American Graffiti*esque things that teenage boys are supposed to do: cruising Van Nuys Boulevard in my white 1959 Chevy Impala with chrome wheels and tuck and roll, trying to pick up girls, drag racing down quiet residential streets, stealing hubcaps, having our hubcaps stolen, picking up girls. Did I mention picking up girls? Yes, like most healthy, red-blooded American boys of Italian/Indian/Irish descent I was girl-crazy.

Not that I was very successful. Remember, I was young, naive, new to the game, and not what you would consider the leading man type. And, unfortunately, most of the girls I became attracted to ended up telling me, "Oh, Micky. I like you like a brother." Don't you hate it when that happens?

But that didn't stop me from trying. And trying. And trying. It wasn't until I was seventeen that I graduated from trying to doing. That's old for a boy, I suppose, but I did make up for it in the long run.

Which reminds me of the only birds-and-the-bees talk I ever got from my father. I was about ten years old and it was one of the very few times I can remember him talking to me about anything personal. I must have asked him something like, "Where do babies come from?" This was his explanation:

"Well, Micky. At night, when Mommy and Daddy are in bed, Daddy's pee-pee goes over to Mommy's pee-pee and leaves a little seed inside. And that seed grows up into a baby."

Fine. Except for one thing. My parents slept in separate beds, like Ozzie and Harriet. And he neglected to tell me that Daddy *first* gets out of his bed and gets into Mommy's bed. For years I waited in dread for the day when my "pee-pee" would turn into this serpent that would snake its way across my room, out the door, and end up God only knows where.

My favorite classes in high school were science, electronics, and history. The rest you could keep. And besides the activities listed above, I played around with ham radio, raised pigeons, and rode my horse around the San Fernando Valley. Coco and I both had horses and we used to raise hell riding up and down the streets. We weren't yelling "Blaackhaawk!" anymore, but the thought was there. (And yes, Coco, Apache *was* faster than Blaze.)

For the most part, my high school years were uneventful (thankfully). One interesting side note: I had been so used to being dressed by a wardrobe department that I had no fashion sense whatsoever. I couldn't have cared less about clothes (I still don't). So rather than having to decide what to wear every day to be cool, I bought half a dozen pairs of black pants and a dozen white shirts and wore virtually the same thing to school every day for three years! Tacky, but convenient.

Well, I finally managed to graduate from high school (barely) and half-heartedly started my university career at Valley Junior College, often described as a high school with ashtrays. I signed up for a full load of classes then gradually dropped them one by one out of disinterest or boredom.

One bright, sunny day in early 1963 I was sitting in Psych 101, listening to what Freud thought about anal something-or-other when a message came from the office; I had an emergency phone call. It was the wife of my father's business partner. All she said was that she was going to be picking me up. Something was obviously very wrong.

When she arrived she said, "Your father would want you to be strong." The first thing that crossed my mind was that my mother had died, but when I got home my mom was standing in the hall, crying. She looked up as I walked in and simply said, "Your father is not with us anymore."

Despite what I've said about his foibles, my dad was a good man, an anachronism—but a good man. Kind, strong of character, passionate, hard-working, driven, and definitely a Type A personality. (He died of a heart attack from years of red wine, red meat, and cigarettes.)

When I was very young we had been very close, building things, working around the house together, playing games. But events conspired against us; my TV series, his TV series, the extraordinary demands the restaurant made on his time and energy, and the natural forces that always seem to polarize the new generation from the previous one. I was not very close to my father when he died. I was off into my world of drag-racing and rock & roll, and he was firmly anchored in his world of veal scallopini and opera. But I loved him, and I was very upset when he died.

But my real anguish lay in what his death did to my mother. I realize that I haven't talked much about my mother. That's simply because good moms tend to be kind of invisible, like furniture. They're just always there, offering comfort, care, taxi service, meals, maintenance, and first aid. The events that stand out in our lives tend to be the dramatic or traumatic, not the domestic and routine.

My mom was the best of moms. She had always been there for me, and it was terrible to see her so distraught. Given my melodramatic bent it is no surprise that I reacted in a dramatic, if not bizarre, way. The first thing I did was write a note to the people of the future that read something like:

"If anyone gets this letter, please bring my father back to life and send him back in time. His death has really upset my mother."

Then I sealed it in a box and buried it in the backyard. (Isaac Asimov would have been proud of me.) The next thing I did was gather up all of the Bibles in the house and burn them! I admit it was an extreme and sacrilegious thing to do, but at the time I was not awfully rational. I figured it this way: If there *was* a God, then I was not too crazy about Him, and, as far as I was concerned, He had a *lot* to answer for.

(This is not the time or place to expound on my philosophy or world view; I'll save that for another book. But, briefly, I believe, as did Buckminster Fuller, that God is a verb. A verb that not only describes the sum total of all natural physical processes but also the workings in the metaphysical worlds of ideas, values, and truth. [Much like Plato's ideal world of mathematical concepts.] We make contact with these worlds of action via the intellect and perceive of them by the exercise of reason, insight, and revelation. In my humble opinion, God did not create the universe, the universe is Godding.)

As you can imagine, my father's death threw the family into a tailspin. My mom suddenly found herself alone, raising four children whose ages ranged from two to seventeen. To make matters worse, my youngest sister, Gina, had just been diagnosed with a severe learning disability. I don't know how my mom coped. But cope she did. We still got the meals, the maintenance, and the taxi service.

For my part, I became rather aimless. I quit school, started cruising around more, and thinking less. And, predictably, my idle hands led to mischief.

Cut To:

Int. Micky's Car—Night

Micky and his buddies, Bill and Fred (the names have been changed to protect the innocent), are hanging out at BOB'S BIG BOY DRIVE-IN in Van Nuys, California. Van Nuys Boulevard is *the* main drag and BOB'S is *the* main hangout. The year is 1964. Micky has traded in the white Chevy for a jet black Pontiac Grand Prix with mag wheels, a four-speed Hurst transmission and a new, groovy, in-car television (the only one on the Boulevard). They have just finished watching the *Ed Sullivan Show* featuring this new group called THE BEATLES. Bill, a "greaser," is not impressed.

BILL

Man, what stupid-looking hair.

FRED

Yeah, but I'll bet they're getting laid.

Micky is cruising through the parking lot checking out the action.

MICKY

Let's blow this joint. There's nothing going on.

FRED

What are we gonna do?

MICKY

I don't know. What do you wanna do, Bill?

Bill is the oldest of the trio, and the other guys often look to him for inspiration. Bill thinks for a minute, then his eyes light up.

BILL

Hey, I got it! Let's go garaging!

MICKY

What's that?

BILL

You'll see. Hit it!

Micky slams the four-speed into first gear, revs the gas-guzzling powerplant up to four grand, and pops the clutch. The big black beast lunges forward, tires smoking, and leaves the hamburger joint far behind in a cloud of vaporized rubber.

Smash Cut To:

Int. Subterranean Garage—Night

The guys are somewhere in Hollywood. They have been "garaging" for a few hours and are stoked on adrenaline. Garaging, it turns out, is simply the act of finding an unlocked car in a secluded apartment garage and taking out anything that isn't bolted down.

The night's work has been *very* lucrative. At last count, the booty has consisted of five flashlights, an empty briefcase, a set of jumper cables, and ten or twenty maps.

Currently they are cleaning out the back of a Jaguar XKE that the owner foolishly left open.

MICKY

Wow! Another map!

Suddenly they freeze. A cop car is cruising by, slowly! The gang of three stands glued to the spot as the gendarmes shine a flashlight into the darkness. But they don't stop! Apparently, they think it's just someone transferring stuff from one car to another. Micky and Fred breathe a sigh of relief but Bill, the "pro," panics.

BILL
(screaming)

COPS!

The cop car screeches to a halt and backs up, red lights flashing. Inside the garage pandemonium reigns.

Fred and Bill dive over the Jag and scramble away. Micky opts for the side exit and is just rounding the corner of the building when the beam of a powerful flashlight blinds him. He stops in his tracks. At the other end of the beam is the silhouette of a man in uniform. One hand is holding the flashlight, the other hand is holding something much more dangerous.

COP

Don't move and put your hands up over your head
. . . slowly

Fade Out

So they booked me into the Beverly Hills sheriff's station, charged me with petty theft, and let me call my mom. She came down with our family lawyer and I met her in the holding area. She was crying. I was so embarrassed and ashamed that I could hardly speak. They told me I would have to stay in jail for the night because it was too late to get me out. I found out later that they had decided, along with the police, that it might be a good idea for me to spend the night in jail. It was. I stayed out of trouble for a long, long time.

The news services did manage to pick up the piece, though, and the next night on the eleven o'clock news the local tabloid reporter opened his report with: "Last night, child star Micky Braddock was caught in a Hollywood scene that wasn't in the act!" Needless to say, I was mortified.

It was during my late teens that I started to drift back into acting. I found an agent who signed me up and started sending me out on interviews. At first it was difficult because the casting people only knew my name in reference to *Circus Boy*, and since I hadn't worked in years, they didn't know what to expect. Some hadn't even bothered to do their homework. Once, when I was eighteen and nearly six feet tall, I showed up at an interview and walked into a room full of ten-year-old blond kids.

But I did some interesting work during those years. I guest starred on *Mr. Novak* and *Owen Marshall;* costarred with Jack Klugman and Art Carney in a *Playhouse 90* written by Rod Serling; and even had a recurring part in *Peyton Place,* playing a punk who beats up Norman Harrington, (played by Christopher Connelly), and then promptly gets beaten up by his brother, played by Ryan O'Neal. Great fun.

It's about now that the music muse started flirting with me again. I'd kept up guitar after *Circus Boy* and even studied classical guitar for a while. But you couldn't go to a party and impress girls by covering Segovia tunes, so I learned the popular songs of the day like "Michael Rowed the Boat Ashore" and "Tom Dooley." Coco (who has a gorgeous voice) and I also started singing together more often, and I started writing songs.

But rock & roll was coming on stronger than ever. And when the Beatles hit the scene the pawnshops were swamped with secondhand classical guitars, including mine. I distinctly remember driving down Ventura Boulevard, listening to the radio, on the way to my day job behind the singles counter at Wallach's Music City when the disc jockey announced it was "B-Day," and "I Wanna Hold Your Hand" was being played every ten minutes. I remember thinking, "Boy, would I like to be in a group like the Beatles." You have to be careful what you pray for.

There were a lot of changes going on in my life during the years, 1964–65. My mom got remarried to a wonderful man named Dr. Robert Scott, a minister, and they decided to move the family up to San Jose. Much to my mom's dismay, I decided to stay in Los Angeles. One of the reasons was that my best friend at the time, Rick Klein (who later became my stand-in on *The Monkees*), had suggested that since both of us were not getting any younger, and neither of us had any career plans, we should go to architecture school and open a remodeling business. It sounded like a great idea.

The other reason I stayed in L.A. (and if the truth be known the *real* reason) was that I was embroiled in my first real love affair with a cute little Valley girl. And she was dumping me. Oh, the rejection! Oh, the pain of unrequited love! Oh, the agony and the ecstasy! I even rented an apartment right across the street from hers so I could watch her come and go and wallow in my misery.

In the meantime, I got more and more involved in music. I'd been hanging out at some of the local nightclubs and eventually gathered up enough courage to get up on stage and sing a few songs. I became known for my distinctive renditions of "Johnny B. Goode," "Money," and "Lucille." ("Distinctive" meaning that I would jump about and scream until I lost my voice.) Every Monday night was amateur night at the Red Velvet Nightclub on the Sunset Strip. I would get up there in my shiny sharkskin suit, razor-cut hairdo, pointy shoes, and do my thing.

One night some guy in an even shinier sharkskin suit came up to me and asked if I wanted to join a band as a lead singer and go on the road! "Who me? Yes, please." A few weeks later I found myself on the way to Denver, Colorado, with four other scruffy musicians to open in a nightclub. We called ourselves Micky and the One-Nighters.

To say that this road trip was different from my touring experiences as Circus Boy would be a gross understatement. Instead of the Waldorf, we stayed in a cockroach-infested apartment above a rancid nightclub. Instead of limos, we rode in a couple of broken-down VW Bugs and a U-Haul trailer. Instead of chocolate éclairs and French onion soup, we ate Hostess Twinkies and chili dogs. I loved it. I even got my first dose of the clap.

I sang my heart out in that band: Animals, Stones, Dave Clark Five, Beatles, Little Richard, Jerry Lee Lewis, Chuck Berry. This was my pre-Monkee singing (I call it my PMS), and if you want to know where the real Micky Dolenz was musically just review that list. I loved the angst of it, the grubbiness, the bounced paychecks, the dirty girls. Sex, Beer, and Rock & Roll! (There weren't any drugs around yet.)

It was 1965 and between singing in the band (we'd changed our name to the Missing Links), trying to keep up my architectural classes at L.A. Trade Technical College, mourning over lost love, and watching the Watts riots, I was a busy boy. But there were big changes blowing in the wind.

One day after the Missing Links had finished playing a week's gig in a local bowling alley cocktail lounge, the band called me up and asked me to come over to the motel where they were staying. I thought it was for a rehearsal. It wasn't.

Cut To:

Int. Crummy Motel Room—Day

The four members of the band, Tom, Dick, Harry, and Steve (names changed to protect the guilty) are sitting around drinking beer and smoking. There's a knock at the door. They glance at each other nervously.

TOM

Come in.

The door swings open and in bounces Micky, bright-eyed and bushy-tailed. He grabs a beer, pops the cap, and starts slugging it down.

MICKY

Hey, what's happening guys?

DICK
(seriously)

We have to talk.

Micky senses something is afoot and sits down. The band members cast furtive looks back and forth. No one speaks. You can cut the tension with a knife.

MICKY

Okay, so what's going on?

Harry, the band leader, stands and starts to pace.

HARRY

The thing is . . . You see . . . Well, we just figure that since you're just singing . . . and we sing . . . and you aren't playing an instrument . . . Well, we thought that we could make more money by cutting the group down in size.

Micky just stares at Harry. No one speaks. You can cut the silence with the same knife.

MICKY

I can start playing guitar. I do play guitar, ya know.

STEVE

We don't need another guitar.

There's really not much more to be said. Micky puts on a brave face, puts down the beer, and quietly leaves the room.

Fade Out

I'd been fired! Canned. Axed. Dismissed. Terminated. I drove back down the smoggy freeway in a daze. I'd never been fired from any job before in my life. I'd never felt that feeling of helpless humility before. And I didn't like it. What now? Keep going to school? Get my architecture license and spend the rest of my life designing other people's bathrooms? For one of the first times in my life I was at a loss.

A couple of days later one of the guys in the band must have been feeling guilty. He calls me up to see how I was doing.

Cut To:

Int. Micky's Apartment—Day

Micky is morose. He's watching TV, pecking at a lukewarm chicken pot pie, and attempting to review a chapter on "The Tensile Strength of Pre-Stressed Concrete." The phone RINGS.

MICKY

Hello?

HARRY (V.O.)

Hey, good buddy. How's it going?

MICKY

Oh, not bad. What's going on with you guys?

HARRY (V.O.)

Not much. We might be getting a gig at a bar mitzvah.

MICKY

Great.

HARRY (V.O.)
(*struggling*)

So . . . What's happening? You have anything coming up?

MICKY

Not a lot . . . Well, actually I did go for an interview yesterday. It was for a TV show.

HARRY (V.O.)
(*relieved*)

Hey, that's great.

MICKY

Yeah. It's called *The Monkees.*

Fade Out

The Magical Monkee Machine

Gaily bedight,

A gallant knight,

In sunshine and in shadow,

Had journeyed long,

Singing a song,

In search of Eldorado.

—Edgar Allan Poe
Eldorado

It's been documented to death how the Beatles and the British invasion in general altered forever the music, art, style, fashion, and socio-political world view of a generation. But to a kid on the streets of L.A. circa 1964, it was simply, "Man, are those guys cool!" The Beatles smoked cigarettes, drank, lounged around like wise old soldiers, and exuded an air of extraordinary sophistication compared to the teen beat, surf-city, Presley pelvic, folky-wolky influences that had dominated the American music and fashion scenes for a decade. That gritty, streetwise sophistication came, primarily, from the fact that the Beatles had grown up in what was essentially a ghetto: postwar Liverpool.

Like almost everyone else, I too was scrambling to jump onto the British bandwagon. I became a major Beatle fan and

remain one to this day. I threw away my can of Aquanet and
my Jay Sebring styling brush. I relegated the sharkskin suits
to the hall closet, and exchanged all my worn-out adjectives
like "boss" and "hip" for the new/improved "fab" and
"gear."

By 1965, the music, television, and film industries in Hollywood and New York were trying desperately to capture the
essence of, and capitalize on, the burgeoning youth scene. Basically, they wanted to coax as many dollar bills out of those tight
little jeans as they could.

During late '64 and early '65 I was up for a number of TV
pilots that were trying to emulate the teen scene. Most were
extremely lame. You could tell that they'd been conceived of and
developed by some fat cat sitting at the top of a glass tower,
smoking a cigar, pronouncing, "Let's do a show the kids will
like."

There was one show in development about a folk group
like Peter, Paul and Mary, another about a Beach Boys–type
surfing group, and yet another styled after the New Christy
Minstrels. Each one was as grim as the next. And then there was
this one show called . . . *The Monkees*.

The Monkees was different right from the get-go. That's
because the guys that had put it together, Bob Rafelson and Bert
Schneider, were very different from the traditional TV producers. They were young, hip, and irreverent—unheard-of charac-
teristics for TV producers of the time, but just the right stuff for
potential purveyors of the new pop subculture.

Bob had created the folk music show *Hootenanny* and had
directed the TV series *The Greatest Show on Earth*. He was being
touted as a new "hot" (if somewhat hard to work with) film-
maker. Bert's father was Abe Schneider, the president of Columbia Pictures, the company that owned Screen Gems. Screen
Gems was the production company that produced *The Monkees*.
What a coinkeydink.

You would have to ask them what their perspective was on all of this, but, from my point of view, here were a couple of guys that were simply trying to get what was *really* happening on the streets onto the national television screens. And not incidentally, of course, make a fortune.

It's often been said that the Monkees were America's answer to the Beatles. Nothing could be further from the truth. That would be like saying *Star Trek* was Hollywood's answer to NASA's space program. No matter what's been said or contended, *The Monkees* was a TV show *about* a group; about *all* the thousands of groups that were budding up around the States at the time, playing in nightclubs, living in one-room hovels, subsisting on Hostess Twinkies and chili dogs. *The Monkees* was more about Micky and the One-Nighters than it was the Beatles. But there was even more to it than that. Funnily enough it was John Lennon who, when asked about the Monkees/Beatles comparisons, said, "I like the Monkees. They're like the Marx Brothers." He was absolutely right. The Monkees were the Marx Brothers with long hair.

I never saw the now infamous "open casting call" classified ad that Bob and Bert placed in the local show-biz trade papers. I had an agent who read about the casting call in *The Breakdowns*, a casting update published daily. Of course, as I had somewhat of a track record, I didn't go to the cattle call (heaven forbid!); I had a *private* audition.

Cut To:

Ext. Columbia Pictures—Day

Micky pulls up to the studio gate in his VW Bug (the Grand Prix was getting too expensive to run). The guard at the gate approaches the car.

GUARD

May I . . . Hey, Micky. Howya doing, kid?

Micky recognizes the guard as the same one who was guarding this particular gate when he and his mom arrived for the *Circus Boy* interview nearly ten years ago to the day.

MICKY

Hi. Can I park in here?

GUARD

Sure, Mick. Say, how's that elephant?

MICKY

He died.

Micky parks the car and enters the producer's building.

Cut To:

Int. Producer's Building—Day

Micky gets a script from the secretary and sits down in a small office lobby. There are three or four other guys also waiting. He recognizes a couple of them from other recent interviews.

SECRETARY

Micky Braddock?

MICKY

Yes?

SECRETARY

They will see you now.

Micky goes through to an inner office and is immediately struck by the unconventional ambience. First of all the place is a mess. There are magazines scattered everywhere, a half-eaten pizza lies on the floor, and stacks of used coffee cups are piled up on the desk. "This kinda looks like my apartment," thinks Micky to himself. He also notices this strange smell, kinda like burning weeds . . .

Micky expects to see an older man in a gray suit sitting behind a desk. Instead, he sees two guys lounging on the couch. They're in their thirties, wearing jeans and T-shirts, and their hair is longer than his! Micky is slightly taken aback but recovers quickly. Some little voice inside him says, "This is different. This is cool. Go for it!"

It's been a couple of seconds since he entered the room and not a word has been spoken. They're checking him out. Micky walks right up to the desk, takes a coffee cup from one of the stacks and deftly places it on the desk.

MICKY

Checkmate . . .

Fade Out

I must have done the right thing because they laughed, and the interview breezed by after that. Bob and Bert asked all the typical questions, but in a delightfully refreshing way, and I read a few scenes from the script, then I left.

A few weeks later I got a call-back. This time the interview was more extensive and I read more scenes from the pilot script. (The character names in this early script were something like, "Biff," "Dicky," "Fred," and "Suds.") Then they told me that they wanted me to do a screen test. I left the building that day on a real high. Something told me that this could be big. I usually didn't get too excited on these interviews, but I definitely re-member thinking, "I really want this one."

Besides going on Monkee call-backs, I was also getting more active in recording. A couple of small-time record produ-cers had heard me singing somewhere and offered to cut a record. I wrote a song called "Don't Do It," and we recorded it in a small studio in Hollywood. To their credit, they put together a real good band of top studio musicians, including this great new guitar player called Glen Campbell. Glen later played on some of the early Monkee tracks and we became friends.

The Monkees screen tests were as unusual as the interviews had been. In retrospect, it's apparent that Bob and Bert weren't trying to "cast" the show in the traditional sense, i.e., attempting to find actors to fit already established roles, but were looking for unique multitalented personalities who would be distinct, dynamic, yet be able to work together without stepping on each other's toes and, hopefully, develop a rapport that would trans-late onto the screen.

Every able-bodied young male on both coasts was up for these roles; including Paul Petersen from *The Donna Reed Show,* Stephen Stills, the group the Lovin' Spoonful, and some say Charles Manson (though I doubt it, but it does make interesting gossip). There was even this young actor/singer named Paul Williams who auditioned for the show. I came to know Paul pretty well in later years, and one day he confided in me that not

The Monkees in 1966, as we will always be remembered: Mike Nesmith, Peter Tork, Davy Jones, and me on the drums. (Actually, this is a trick photo, *we're* the ones that are upside down, not Davy.) (RAYBERT PRODUCTIONS/MJB ARCHIVES)

Dad was the star of TV's *The Count of Monte Cristo* in the fifties. (MICKY DOLENZ COLLECTION)

My father, George Dolenz, with Susanna Foster in the 1944 film *The Magic Voice*. (UNIVERSAL PICTURES/MICKY DOLENZ COLLECTION)

Mom had her own turn as a screen ingenue in the forties. (JANELLE SCOTT COLLECTION)

My family in the late forties: Dad, me, Mamoo, Uncle Jack, Coco, and Mom. (MICKY DOLENZ COLLECTION)

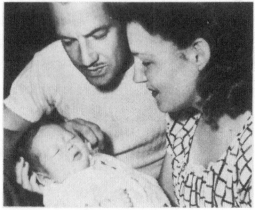

When I was born in 1945, Dad's movie studio sent out this publicity shot of my parents and me. (UNIVERSAL PICTURES/MICKY DOLENZ COLLECTION)

Pudgy but cute. Notice the almond eyes, courtesy of some dim and distant Indian gene infusion. (MICKY DOLENZ COLLECTION)

Stalking my neighborhood nemesis: Edgar the bully. (MICKY DOLENZ COLLECTION)

In my award-winning costume as the "History of Halloween" (or, rather, my mom's award-winning costume with me as runway model). (MICKY DOLENZ COLLECTION)

Coco and me in 1957. (MICKY DOLENZ COLLECTION)

My little sisters, Gina and Debbie, in 1964. (MICKY DOLENZ COLLECTION)

All dressed up, with Mom and Coco on our way to see my first (and last) opera, *La Bohème*. (MICKY DOLENZ COLLECTION)

Poolside in 1958. (MICKY DOLENZ COLLECTION)

This cute little chimp is the same rotten little sucker that mistook my finger for a banana. (© 1956, 1993 CPT HOLDINGS, COLUMBIA PICTURES TELEVISION/MJB ARCHIVES)

The horse is full grown, I'm on stilts. (© 1956, 1993 CPT HOLDINGS, COLUMBIA PICTURES TELEVISION/BY CROSBY/MJB ARCHIVES)

With Noah Beery as my Uncle Joey the Clown, and Robert Lowery as Big Tim Champion. (© 1956, 1993 CPT HOLDINGS, COLUMBIA PICTURES TELEVISION/JOE RUSSO COLLECTION)

In the plot of the show, my parents were killed in an acrobatic accident, and Uncle Joey became my guardian. (© 1956, 1993 CPT HOLDINGS, COLUMBIA PICTURES TELEVISION/BY CROSBY/MICKY DOLENZ COLLECTION)

Uncle Joey is pulling "a fast one"
on Big Tim Champion while I
pick my nose. (© 1956, 1993 CPT
HOLDINGS, COLUMBIA PICTURES
TELEVISION/MICKY DOLENZ
COLLECTION)

Dressed as a pirate for
a dream sequence on
Circus Boy. (MICKY
DOLENZ COLLECTION)

Starring in *Circus Boy* was an incredible
experience for me. It was like living in a real
live circus for three years. (© 1956, 1993 CPT
HOLDINGS, COLUMBIA PICTURES TELEVISION/JOE
RUSSO COLLECTION)

Hey, hey, we're the Monkees! (RHINO RECORDS/MARK BEGO COLLECTION)

With Mike and Peter in San Juan Capistrano the week we launched the TV series. Davy was having a bad hair day. (RAYBERT PRODUCTIONS/MJB ARCHIVES)

One of the first publicity shots, taken on the set of the pilot. Sal Mineo, eat your heart out. (RAYBERT PRODUCTIONS/MJB ARCHIVES)

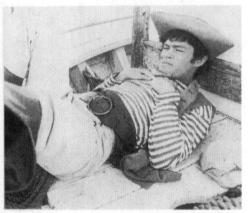

Being a pirate was becoming a recurring theme for me! (HENRY DILTZ)

For me, recording songs for the TV show was just part of my job as one of the Monkees; a delightful part. (HENRY DILTZ)

Is this just another episode of *The Monkees* or another meeting with my ex-wife? (RAYBERT PRODUCTIONS/MJB ARCHIVES)

This particular expression is Grimace #32-R and took years to perfect. I learned it in Stupid Looks 101. (RAYBERT PRODUCTIONS/MJB ARCHIVES)

Monkees as Mavericks. From the pilot. (RAYBERT PRODUCTIONS/MJB ARCHIVES)

Monkees as models for JCPenney. God, what geeky clothes! (RAYBERT PRODUCTIONS/STEVE COX COLLECTION)

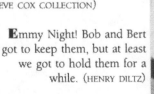

Emmy Night! Bob and Bert got to keep them, but at least we got to hold them for a while. (HENRY DILTZ)

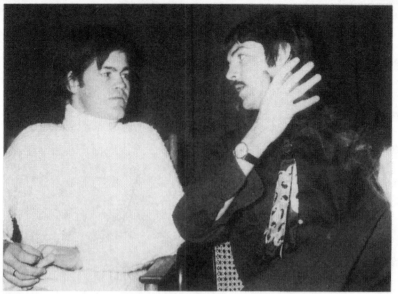

Monkee meets Beatle! I've just asked Paul for his autograph, and he is about to smack me across the face. (*LONDON DAILY MIRROR*)

All aboard on the Magical Monkee Tour. Please keep your brains inside your head at all times. (HENRY DILTZ)

"All right, Bert. I'll sing, I'll sing. Just don't hit me again." (HENRY DILTZ)

Hey! What do you know? I've been playing this thing upside down all this time! (HENRY DILTZ)

only had he been up for *The Monkees* but had also been up for *Circus Boy!*

The one screen test turned into other screen tests. And at each stage they got more involved and more demanding. These weren't just acting exercises anymore. Casting *The Monkees* was much like casting a Broadway musical. They were obviously looking for multitalented performers. We had to act, sing, dance, improvise, and play an instrument. My musical audition piece was "Johnny B. Goode," on the guitar.

I was pretty comfortable with all of it, except the improvising. As an actor I was so used to working with a script that trying to make things up as I went along made me very nervous. But Bob Rafelson was very patient and I finally got the hang of it.

There were about thirty guys in the first wave of screen tests and that number soon dropped to just eight or ten. It was pretty nerve-racking going through that process. I would finish a day's testing, go home, and wait by the phone, sometimes for days, until I got a call from my agent. Every time the phone rang I was expecting him to say something like, "They've decided to go in a different direction" (which is Hollywoodese for "You're out.").

It was during one of these early tests that I must have met the other guys who were eventually to become The Monkees: Michael Nesmith, Peter Tork, and Davy Jones, but I don't remember them distinctly. At the time, of course, there were dozens of other "contestants," and I doubt if the other guys remembered me either. When it finally got down to the final eight I do remember working a lot with Davy. Bob and Bert must have thought that we had some sort of chemistry happening because they often paired us up. (They were right, Davy and I worked together like magic.)

One day I got the call. I had been chosen to do the pilot! Now, you might think that I would have gone ape (excuse the pun), but I took it quite calmly. I knew, after all, that a pilot was just a pilot, and that dozens of pilots went unsold every year. It was a long way from a pilot deal to a network sale, so I would just hang in there and hope for the best.

The four of us Monkees met for the first time as a unit during a wardrobe fitting. Looking back now it seems kind of funny, but there we were, four strangers, introducing ourselves to each other like we had just boarded the same plane. "Hello, I'm Micky Braddock." "Hi, I'm Davy Jones, nice to see you again," . . . etc. The airplane metaphor is quite apt, actually, considering the destination, altitude, and speed of the trip we were all about to take together.

My first impressions of the other guys was a lasting one and hasn't really changed much over the years:

MIKE NESMITH: Dry, witty sense of humor, intelligent, cool, generous, somewhat insecure, and definitely a control freak. One of the funniest men I have ever known.

PETER TORK: Bohemian, heart of gold, tortured, compassionate, sometimes annoying, intellectual, altruistic, and one of the kindest men I have ever known.

DAVY JONES: Stylish, very talented, very short, puckish, unselfish, somewhat vain, congenial, streetwise, and one of the nicest men I have ever known.

It was at this time that I was informed I was going to be the drummer. I said, "But I don't play the drums." Bob and Bert explained to me that since Mike and Peter were already very accomplished on guitar and bass, and Davy was obviously supposed to be the cute "lead singer," I had been cast as the drummer. Well, I was a professional, mine was not to reason why. I had learned to ride an elephant for one series, why not learn to play the drums for another? Anyway, I told them I couldn't play keyboards because it made my butt hurt.

It wasn't long after that we went down to San Diego—to Del Mar—to film the pilot. That was a gas. Everything I'd hoped for was coming true. The script was funny, new, and outrageous.

The slightly irreverent, off-the-wall spirit that had been in evidence even in my first interview was still the modus operandi.

The atmosphere on the set was exciting and stimulating. And, mainly, it was young. We were young, the producers were young, the crew was young. They hired a wonderful commercial director named Mike Elliot who added a stylized visual look, and the two writers who had co-created the show and written the pilot were standing by to rewrite any scenes that needed it. Their names were Larry Tucker and Paul Mazursky.

Meanwhile, we were already trying it out as a band. I was at a distinct disadvantage because I was attempting to play an unfamiliar instrument, but I gave it my best shot. Even on the set of that pilot we fired up the instruments between takes and jammed on some rock & roll tune or other. I must have been terrible. But everyone, especially Peter, was very supportive.

For the pilot, the actual soundtrack music had previously been recorded and all we really had to do was play along with it. It was challenging but exciting. I felt just the way Sal Mineo must have in *The Gene Krupa Story*.

After the pilot was filmed, we just went home and waited. And that was the toughest time of all. Everyone had worked so hard, spent so much time, spent so much money; and all it would take would be one network executive in New York, one of those fat cats with a cigar, to say, "Nay, I don't like it," and it would have all been in vain.

I was not privy to those network meetings, of course, but I understand that the Monkees pilot *was* originally rejected. It had tested badly and the networks had turned it down. Then, I'm told, Bob Rafelson insisted upon going back into the editing room and recutting the show.

Bob and Bert made a couple of brave decisions during that period. One was to cut *in* segments of our original screen tests, and the other was to cut *out* one of the main characters that had been written into the show . . . the Manager. Yes, the Monkees were originally going to have a manager/mentor who was going to look after them. Kind of a *Manager Knows Best.* This was undoubtedly due to the pressure from the Standards and Practices department at the network.

After all, "you couldn't just have young people running around on their own, being masters of their own destiny!" You had to have an adult authority figure in control, albeit in the background, but always around to steer the poor misguided youths through their problems and protect them from their own devices.

But Bob cut the manager out and that was probably the smartest thing he ever did. Now the Monkees were on their own, autonomous, carefree, honorable, and unfettered by any adult, establishment figures. Whatever he did, it must have worked. One day I got a call from Bert Schneider. NBC had ordered twenty-six episodes of the show. We were on the air!

Now I really had my work cut out for me. I started practicing the drums with a passion. I bought this little rubber practice pad and I took it everywhere. It drove everyone crazy. The producers set up a small rehearsal area on one of the empty soundstages, and in between the photo shoots, wardrobe fittings, press interviews, and production meetings we would go off and rehearse. (Those early sessions must have been abominable!)

Because of our similar backgrounds, Davy and I had a lot in common and hit it off almost immediately. We were used to the film production process and took to it like lawyers to politics. Mike and Peter, on the other hand, were more familiar with the worlds of recording and performing, and they blossomed whenever we started to rehearse or record.

Unfortunately, even from the very beginning, it was apparent that Mike and Peter were destined for confrontation. There really couldn't be two more incompatible characters. Mike is pragmatic, Peter is ethereal. Peter is laid-back, Mike is impatient. Mike is oil, Peter is water. There's no way these two would have ever gotten together to form a group under normal circumstances but, here we were, all together in a small room, in the final stages of labor, trying to give birth to something that resembled music.

The problem really came down to this: Mike and Peter each had a very strong, clear vision of where the group should go musically. And they were very different visions. They would have these endless artistic duels about the "sound," and the "groove," and the "feel." Davy and I would look at each other, shrug, and go have a beer.

In fairness to both of them, it was apparent right from the beginning that the producers had promised *both* of them that they would be able to express their particular brand of music under the Monkees' banner. But there really can be only one leader of a band, one musical perspective; like there can be only one painter of a picture. (Partnerships like Lennon and McCartney are the exceptions.) The Monkees (as just the four of us) simply never had this singularity of musical vision. The reason I'm going on about this now is that it's important to appreciate how and when this seed of disparity was planted; because it would eventually grow into the weed that would ultimately strangle the group.

But musical differences aside, when we walked onto the set to film the show, it was magic! Through design or dumb luck, the producers had managed to pick four personalities that just hit it off, big time! They must have cast the show with their hearts instead of their heads, because the chemistry was definitely there. It was as if we had been working together for years.

Even in the early episodes we were starting to ad-lib the dialogue, much to Bob and Bert's pleasure and surprise. Unlike a normal TV show, they decidedly did *not* want us to stick faithfully to the script. They encouraged, nay *urged* us, to be spontaneous, zany, wacky, and off-the-wall. We would get a script each week and review it, but when we got on the set, anything went. If the scene involved other actors and some important plot points, then we would try to hold it down, but if we were left on our own, you just never knew what was going to happen. And it's no coincidence that many of the shots they used in editing together the episodes came from these moments—moments that would have been considered unusable outtakes by others.

The comedy was certainly our strong point and most of it came naturally, but we *had* worked on it. After all, "comedy is no laughing matter." Before we had started filming Bob and Bert had sat us down and screened movies by the Marx Brothers, Laurel and Hardy, the Three Stooges, the Bowery Boys, and the Beatles for us. But they didn't want us to *emulate* anyone else, they wanted us to develop our own personalities and, if anything, become caricatures of ourselves.

Peter had the toughest job. The Harpo Marx–type character he played on *The Monkees* is entirely different from his actual personality. As for Mike and Davy and me, we just became more of the same: wittier, cuter, and zanier, respectively.

At first the improvising was hard for me. I was used to working with a script and simply hadn't been trained in that discipline. They brought in a young actor named James Frawley to work with us. He had been at Second City with Mike Nichols and Elaine May, and we took to him right away. We would do all these strange exercises like throwing an imaginary ball around or making up characters on the spot. Mike was a natural at this and I learned a lot from watching him. He and I eventually became masters of the spontaneous goof. Jim Frawley would go on to direct the great majority of *The Monkees* episodes.

On the home front, I was still living in the Valley, and had rented a more "up-market" apartment. But what with the filming, the rehearsing, and the recording, I never saw much of it. Unfortunately, I once again lost contact with most of my friends (sort of comes with the territory, I guess).

Just like during *Circus Boy*, the set became my second home. In fact, it can be argued that a movie set is my *first* home.

To this day, when I walk onto a film set I breathe a sigh of relief and a little voice inside says, "Ahhh, home at last."

The studio publicity machine was starting to gear up for the imminent premiere of the series on NBC. The air date was to be September 12, 1966. Things really started hotting up, and when we weren't busy shooting or recording or rehearsing, we were busy taking pictures or doing promotions. Los Angeles radio station KHJ was playing "Last Train To Clarksville" every hour on the hour, so there was already a bit of buzz around town. We'd done some local stuff with the Teen Fair and had appeared in person at the Broadway Theater in New York. Then some bright brainbox in the publicity department organized this big promotional launch called the Last Train to Clarksville.

First they rent a sixteen-car passenger train. Then they manage to have the southern Californian coastal town of San Juan Capistrano change its name for a day to Clarksville. On September 11, the day before the show premiers, they fill the train with members of the local press corps and hordes of local teenagers, presumably bribing the kids with the promise of a free train ride and all the Coke they can drink, and the press corps with the promise of gin martinis. The inside of the train is covered with wall-to-wall photos of, guess who? And set up in one of the box cars is a small stage area complete with our instruments and amps and a PA system.

So the train heads off down the line and everyone starts asking, "So, where are these Monkee guys?" The train gets to Capistrano and stops, they off-load the kids and the reporters and tell them to watch the skys! Everyone looks up and sees a helicopter come in and land on the beach. Out of the copter jumps, guess who? We run to the waiting train, hop aboard, and take up our places behind our waiting instruments.

Unfortunately, the bright brainbox who had conjured up this public relations extravaganza had neglected to analyze what effects a moving freight train would have on the operation of sophisticated audio equipment and the stability of a free-floating set of drums. It was the first time we had played in public, and it was awful.

One day, just before we were to begin shooting the series, we were told that the "Monkeemobile" was finished and was being delivered! I was thrilled. I'd often dropped by Dean Jefferies' auto shop to watch the work in progress and had been waiting with bated banana breath for the debut of our super-duper custom Monkeemobile. The basic body had been a 1966 Pontiac GTO, but by the time the automotive artists had finished their transfigurations, there was little left that anyone at GM would have recognized.

Cut To:

Ext. Studio Lot—Day

The four MONKEES, the production staff, the crew, and the executives are all gathered in the parking lot of the studio for the big moment. Suddenly, someone shouts!

SOMEONE

Here it comes!

Sure enough, down the street we can see something big and RED rolling through the guard gate. As it gets closer we can hear the RUMBLING and rocking of the powerful engine; see the sleek, low lines of the customized body—see the sun REFLECTING off the bright chrome header pipes. An enormous high-perform-ance blower sits on the hood and shrieks.

BLOWER
(shrieking)

"Here I come, screaming down the street . . ."

DEAN JEFFERIES, the designer, is piloting the great beast and pulls it up to a stop in front of the waiting Monkees, who gather around like kids at Christmas. They're ogling and drooling over the plush tan upholstery and the deep red pearlescent paint job when Mike notices something attached to the back of the car.

MIKE

What's that?

Everyone looks over to where he is pointing. In all the excitement, no one has noticed the low, windowless, wooden TRAILER that is attached to the back of the Monkeemobile. The Monkees approach it curiously.

MICKY

Hey, what's this?

PETER

It looks like a big doghouse.

The executives and production staff shift about nervously. It's obvious that something's up but no one is brave enough to come clean. An uneasy silence fills the air.

Finally, a junior staffer is prodded out and steps forward; the sacrificial lamb thrown to the wolves.

STAFFER

It's a surprise.

MIKE
(*suspiciously*)

A surprise?

STAFFER

Yeah. It's great. Look.

He leans forward, grabs the handle of a big LEVER that's sticking out of the "doghouse," and pulls it. Instantly, the sides collapse, swing out to form a ramp, and the roof folds back to form a sort of backdrop.

STAFFER
(*enthusiastically*)

See? It's a stage!

DAVY
(*incredulously*)

A stage?

STAFFER
(*nervously*)

Yeah . . . A stage. That way when you arrive at, say, the grand opening of a *supermarket* you can . . .

That's as far as he gets. As if on cue, the Monkees exchange glances, turn on their heels, and march off. They manage to get about ten feet away before they burst out into hysterical laughter.

Fade Out

We must have laughed for two days. Needless to say, we never saw the Monkeedoggiehouse again. I've often wondered what ever happened to it.

The next few months were absolutely crazy. The average workday would go something like this:

6:30 A.M.	Get up at the last possible minute. Eat a cold Pop Tart, drink a glass of slightly fizzy orange juice, and get dressed on the way to the car.
7:00 A.M.	Arrive at the studio and go into makeup. An old hairdresser, who's been around since silent movies, puts my hair up into curlers. Read last-minute script changes.
7:30 A.M.	Get called on to the set by the assistant director. Run around like an idiot until noon. Flirt with a cute blond actress and get her phone number.
12:00 noon	Have lunch—either a greasy hamburger at the Columbia Bar and Grill or some indescribable slop in the studio cafeteria. Usually meet with some production assistant about some production thing.
1:00 P.M.	Arrive back on the set and go into makeup for a touch up. Run around like an idiot until seven o'clock. In between scenes, take some production stills, greet some relatives of some studio executive who's trying to score points. Notice that Davy is also getting the number of the cute blond actress.
7:00 P.M.	Wrap. Remove makeup (sometimes). Get an even greasier hamburger to go at Norms in Hollywood

and eat it in the car on the way to the RCA recording studios.

7:30 P.M.   Record the vocals for the new songs in the show. Do a live telephone interview with a reporter in Tokyo who can't speak English.

10:30 P.M. Finish recording. Call the cute blond actress. With any luck, I've got to her before Davy has.

11:00 P.M. Take cute blond actress out to dinner. Suggest we stop by my place and listen to my new Bill Cosby album. With any luck she agrees.

1:00 A.M.   With any luck . . .

3:00 A.M.   Take cute blond actress home. Drive back to my apartment with one eye closed.

3:30 A.M.   Look over my lines for the next day. Fall asleep on the couch.

It's no wonder that sometimes I can't remember too much about what went on during those months. But I'm told I had a great time.

In the autumn of 1966, Davy and I decided to rent a place together. We found this wonderful old house up in the Hollywood Hills and moved in. One day, we were just pulling up in front of the house when the disc jockey on KHJ announced, "And now, here's the new one from that fabulous new group . . . The Monkees!" "Last Train to Clarksville" came blasting out of the car radio. Davy and I just looked at each other and beamed.

The record had been released a few weeks before the show's first air date and was receiving an enormous push from the record company, the television company, the network, everybody.

The show premiered on NBC on September 12, 1966, and we all went up to Bert Schneider's house to watch it together. There were a lot of people there, including my heartthrob of all time, Natalie Wood. I'd like to say that I knew her well but, alas,

I could only stand and gaze upon her radiance from afar.

We all watched the show with great interest even though we'd filmed it months before and had seen it a dozen times. The important thing was—what were the ratings going to be? We weren't disappointed. Even though the show started out with only moderate numbers it was soon number one in its time slot. We had a Hit! By the end of October, the show *and* the first Monkees album were number one.

Well, you can imagine, I was pleased as punch. Who wouldn't be? I was hearing my voice all over the radio and watching myself every Monday night on television. I was somewhat blasé about the TV show (I'd been there before), but I was over the moon about the records. Given the level of my success, it was amusing how naive I was about that part of the business. Tommy Boyce (one of the writer/producers) tells the story about how he ran up to me one day and said, "Micky, do you believe it? You've got *three* top ten records in *Billboard!*" I said, "Great . . . What's *Billboard?*"

Except for what I heard on the set, or through my family and friends, I really had no idea of what was going on out there in the big wide world. My days were full, my nights were full, my weekends were full. I hardly slept, I hardly ate, I spent virtually all of my time on the soundstage or in the recording studio or in the rehearsal hall or in my car. It wasn't until late that year that I really became aware of the scale of our success.

It was toward the end of the year and someone had made a mistake and given me a day off. I was running around like crazy to get some Christmas shopping done when I found myself at my local shopping mall in the San Fernando Valley, the same shopping mall I'd shopped at every Christmas, all my life.

I pulled into the parking lot, jumped out of the car, and ran into the building. I was busy concentrating on my shopping list and hadn't got more than fifty feet inside when I heard screams! I looked up and saw dozens of people running toward me. "Shit! A fire," I thought to myself. I turned to run out of the door but was surrounded. They weren't trying to get out, they were trying to get *me!* I barely made it out with my life. *And* never got my shopping done. There was no doubt about it . . . . I had arrived.

S i x

Lights—
Cameras—
Madness

The only infallible criterion

of wisdom to vulgar

judgements—success.

—Edmund Burke
*Letter to a member of the
French National Assembly*

I've often been asked, "What do you think it was that made *The Monkees* so successful?" I've done a lot of thinking about that over the years, especially when I was working in England as a producer and director and trying to launch successful shows of my own, and here is my theory: There isn't just one factor that guarantees the success of any project, television or otherwise; there are always many contributing elements: talent, resources, skill, hard work, organization, perseverance, determination, and even serendipity. *The Monkees* was no exception. But there are no guarantees, no fail-safe formulas. If there were, there would be no failures, no bombs. *Every* show would be a hit show. That's obviously not the case.

But there are some things you can do to increase your

chances of success, and you can certainly avoid things that have proved to be unsuccessful in the past.

In the case of *The Monkees*, there was first of all the construction of the show itself. Beneath all the pop style, zany humor, hip dialogue, fancy editing, special effects, and trendy fashions, there was basically a very conventional dramatic form. There were the good guys, the Monkees, and there were the bad guys: the Evil Count, the Wicked King, the Greedy Landlord, the Bang of Bullies, the Nasty Kidnapper, the Treacherous Spy, etc. Every week the good guys would do battle with the bad guys and at the end of the show, when everything looked utterly hopeless, the good guys would pull the plot out of the fire through the use of brains, brawn, or good luck. This formula is as old as Sophocles and hasn't changed much in the over twenty-four hundred years since.

Then there was this element of youth-in-control that I mentioned earlier. *The Monkees* was the first television show to depict young people on their own, as masters of their own destiny and, what's more, actually doing a good job of it: taking in orphans, defending the weak, helping little old ladies across the street, etc.

And there was the hair. It may seem like a small thing but, believe it or not, one of the reasons *The Monkees* barely made it onto the air was because of our long hair! It's hard to imagine now, but in 1966 long hair was synonymous with everything from radical anti-American subversiveness to crimes against nature. The network and the sponsers were seriously concerned about being seen to tolerate, if not condone, what was considered by most red-blooded Americans to be disgusting demeanor and very antisocial behavior. But, to their everlasting credit, they took the shot. And the kids loved it.

In his book *The Politics of Ecstasy,* Timothy Leary describes the effect *The Monkees* had on altering the consciousness of the American viewing public. To paraphrase:

Suddenly, every Monday night, right in the middle of our

living rooms, in bounced the Monkees. Four harmless, long-haired weirdos who were not only honest, virtuous, clean, and wholesome . . . they were funny! "Look, Mom," said the kids in Peoria, "the Monkees have long hair, and *they* don't rape children and sodomize animals."

It was true. The fact was, we were just behaving like the great majority of kids were behaving all across the country—all across the world: sometimes impetuous, occasionally rebellious, mostly harmless, and always passionate. Just like Greek drama, teenage behavior hasn't changed much for two thousand years either, regardless of the culture. Only the fashions change to project their identity.

The Monkees also stuck to the tried and true recipe that has constituted virtually every successful sitcom from *I Love Lucy* to *The Bill Cosby Show*. Domesticity. *The Monkees* was *My Three Sons* without Fred MacMurray. We lived together in the same house, like brothers—and were faced with the same domestic problems that face most families: money, housekeeping, jobs, romance, and so on. The fact that we solved some of our problems by changing into Monkeemen, or solved others by snapping our fingers and making someone disappear (Monkee ex machina) was irrelevant. The situation was classic and the producers were careful to maintain its integrity.

And if you watch and listen closely, you realize that even for all its pop zaniness, the Monkee humor—the jokes, the slapstick—was all quite conventional (like the Marx Brothers). And *most* important, the humor was neither topical nor satirical. So it never dated. In my opinion, this is one of the primary reasons why the show has fared so well over the years.

And there was us, of course. The four, frenzied, funny fellows that Bob and Bert had picked to star in their show. Naturally, I think they made *wonderful* choices in their casting selections.

Then there was the music. Whether or not you liked the productions, or the vocals, or the "feel," or the "groove" of the

Monkees songs, the fact of the matter was that they were great tunes. If they weren't, they simply wouldn't have stood up for over twenty-five years.

One day, Lester Sill, the West Coast head of Screen Gems publishing, invited me up to the offices to meet the stable of songsmiths that was going to be writing *The Monkees* tunes. Back in those days, before the era of the singer/songwriter, Tin Pan Alley still existed, regularly pumping out quality material for aspiring recording artists.

He took me down a long hallway. On each side of the hall were doors. It looked a lot like a doctor's office. He knocked on the first door and a feminine voice said, "Come in." He opened the door and introduced me to Carole King. She was sitting there in this little cubicle playing a piano into a reel-to-reel tape recorder. We chatted for a moment about the new tune she was writing for me, then he shut the door, and we continued down the hall to visit the other inmates of this musical institution.

Knock-knock, "Micky, meet David Gates."

Knock-knock, "Micky, meet Carole Bayer Sager."

Knock-knock, "Micky, meet Diane Hilderbrand."

And besides these staff writers, there were others; Neil Diamond, Paul Williams, Tommy Boyce and Bobby Hart, John Stewart, Neil Sedaka, Leiber and Stoller, Michael Murphey, Harry Nilsson.

These people don't write too many duff tunes. Is it any wonder that the songs have lasted for so long?

The powers-that-be in Hollywood and New York (hereafter referred to as the PTB) had done their research. They knew precisely the demographics of the audience they wanted to reach—the ten to fifteen year olds. These were the kids who had the most money to spend, and not much to spend it on. The Beatles already belonged to their older sisters and brothers, and they wanted a group of their own. Anyway, the Beatles had left a sort of vacuum when they evolved from "I Wanna Hold Your Hand" to the much more sophisticated *Rubber Soul* and *Sgt.*

Pepper's Lonely Hearts Club Band. These up-and-coming teeny-boppers didn't have anything to listen to that they could appreciate, understand, or relate to—until the Monkees. The void was there, and we filled it . . . very successfully.

Soon, I found myself recording most of the up-tempo lead vocals. I honestly don't know how this came about, but I suspect it was mostly by default. Davy had a very strong, but Broadway theatrical, voice from his training in musical comedy. Mike had a unique, but country western, flavor to his voice and his songs. Peter was into heavy folk rock and (kind soul that he is) had a recurring problem with pitch. So, guess who was left?

Not that I minded, of course. I loved recording. I took to it like a lawyer to a car wreck. I soon became known as "One-Take Dolenz" and used to pride myself in being able to hit notes that only dogs could hear.

Not that I was personally into all the songs that I was being asked, or told, to sing. Remember, I was a major Beatle fan and probably would have much preferred to be doing *Sgt. Pepper* myself, or the Stones, or the Animals. But this was my job and I had to believe that the PTB knew what they were doing. (They obviously did. The first album sold over 5 million copies in America alone and was number one for thirteen weeks.)

No, between Colgems Records and RCA Records and NBC and Screen Gems and Columbia Pictures and God knows who else, they knew they were on to a good thing and were going to milk it for everything that it was worth. And we were along for the ride, whether we liked it or not. But there was trouble afoot, "right here in River City."

It didn't take a rocket scientist to notice that there were problems abrewing very early on. Even though I didn't think it was any of my business at the time, I could sense that Mike Nesmith was not a happy camper. He used to talk about things like "musical integrity" and "creative control," concepts that had just never occurred to me in terms of my capacity as an actor. To me, it would have been like Dennis Quaid wanting to rewrite "Great Balls of Fire," or Val Kilmer deciding he didn't want to sing "Light My Fire."

Mike fought hard to be involved in the recordings. He put together his own studio group and got a couple of his songs on the first album, and was encouraging the rest of us to do the same. It wasn't all altruistic, mind you. He knew full well what the economic potential was of writing a number one hit song, and he wanted his chance.

The PTB managed to appease him for a while by letting him produce and sing a few songs on the early albums, but it was only the beginning of the troubles. The seed that had been planted back in the rehearsal hall had now germinated and was beginning to sprout!

Meanwhile, back at the ranch, I was having troubles of my own. One day I received this very official-looking letter in the mail. It was from the Selective Service. I was being drafted!

Very early on in the audition process the producers had inquired about my draft status. Naturally, they were concerned about committing an enormous amount of time and money to an actor, and a series, only to see their plans and hard work foiled by Uncle Sam's need for fresh cannon fodder.

But I had assured them all along that there was nothing to worry about. Naturally, I was against the war (anybody with a brain was), but I had always been assured by my doctors and lawyers that, because of my childhood bout with Perthese disease, I would never be accepted. So much for doctors and lawyers.

Cut To:

Int. Draft Board Examination Building—Day

The place is teeming with virile young men. Most are nervous, some are anxious, a few are scared to death.

Micky enters the building with his papers and medical charts. He has been well briefed by his doctors and lawyers. He is confident but not arrogant. He goes into the changing room, strips down naked, and follows the herd into the first examination room. There, they are ordered to line up in a big circle. In the center of the circle, a very NASTY MAN in an army-issue lab coat struts about. On his face, a look of utter disdain.

NASTY MAN
(contemptuously)

All right, you "men." Listen up! You see those glass jars over there across the room? I want you to piss in them.

MICKY

From here?

Big mistake. It gets a laugh from the rest of the naked men, but NASTY MAN is not amused. Micky pays for it when it comes time for the hernia examination.

Cut To:

Int. Interview Office—Day

Micky is ushered into the small room and is greeted by a PERSONABLE MAN in uniform who takes his file and starts to review it carefully. Micky sits by attentively, being careful not to appear too cavalier.

PERSONABLE MAN
(*thoughtfully*)

Uh-huh . . . uh-huh.
(*pause*)
So you had Perthese disease as a child, is that right Mr. Dolenz?

MICKY

Yes, sir. I'm afraid my right leg is about a quarter of an inch shorter than my left one.
(*regretfully*)

I guess that means I'm not eligible, right?

The Personable Man reaches for a large rubber stamp.

PERSONABLE MAN

Naaah, no problem. We'll just make sure you fight on hills . . .

MICKY
(*stunned*)

But . . .

PERSONABLE MAN

Next!

Fade Out

Needless to say, I was somewhat distressed. And the producers of *The Monkees* were frantic.

Don't get me wrong, I can be as patriotic as the next man, when the issue is clearly justified and the intentions honorable. The Vietnam War was an abomination. We knew it then and we know it now. In my humble opinion, to avoid military service at *that* time was, indeed, the moral thing to do.

Fortunately for me, I never had to make it an issue. I didn't have to burn my draft card or buy a map of Canada. It turned out that I really wasn't eligible after all. A few weeks later, and much to everyone's relief, I received notice that I had been turned down because I was too skinny! Thank goodness for all those late nights and Hostess Twinkies.

It's time to mention the other two "silent" members of the Monkees, Tommy Boyce and Bobby Hart. Their influence on the early Monkee records can not be overemphasized. They not only wrote and produced some of our biggest hits but were hugely responsible for the Monkee "sound" that was to drive those hits home.

They had actually auditioned for the show at one point, but when the producers decided to "go in another direction," instead of just being discarded, their talents were recognized and exploited.

I gather that they weren't the first choice for producers, though. The bigwigs in the big offices wanted to marry the Monkees to some big players in the business, and we soon found ourselves auditioning for potential producers. But it wasn't easy finding someone to take the project on. First of all, we'd only just met, and we had a long way to go to becoming a viable musical act. Second of all, the hybrid nature of the project, a cross between a real live band and television show, made many uneasy, and there were some big-time producers, like Mickey Most, who turned us down flat.

But the Monkees were right up Tommy and Bobby's proverbial street (they had already produced the music for the pilot), and they took to the venture like lawyers to malpractice suits. They worked very closely with me right from the start: picking tunes, finding keys, working lyrics, directing me in the studio. As far as I was concerned, they *were* the music. Mike and Peter were off doing their thing, and I supported them, but I was quite happy selling millions of units, thank you, and decorating my walls with shiny Gold records. I was very proud of what I was doing.

It wasn't until years later that I fully realized the kind of impact that we'd had on the industry—some positive, some negative. There were rumors going around, of course, about the Monkees being fabricated, and studio created, but when you have a number one show *and* number one records week after week, you really don't give a shit about the criticism.

The confusion, as I see it, was simply that we had broken very new entertainment ground and there were only a few enlightened souls in the media and in the industry in general who had any idea what we were up to.

This was the first time that the television, recording, and radio industries had made a coordinated, concerted assault on the consumer and, frankly, it took many by surprise. Today, in the world of MTV, this is all common or garden-variety stuff. But back then, in the eyes of the "hipoisie," we were like beings from another planet, coming down to rape their women, kill their buffalo, and steal all their airtime.

In addition, because we had our records playing on this hit TV show every Monday night, we had effectively bypassed the traditional mechanism for getting a hit record on the air. There was such a demand for the records that the radio stations *had* to play them. The record stores *had* to stock them and the record promoters *had* to promote them—whether they all liked it or not. It's no wonder that some of these people became jealous and hostile.

I can see how all of this might have upset a few applecarts but, in all respect to these professionals, none of it really bothered me at all—I was too busy being successful. And I contend that the *really* interesting story about the Monkees is the fact that, even though we started out as a TV show *about* a group, we actually did *become* a group—in every sense of the word. After the initial starting up phase, we eventually did it all. All the recordings, all the concerts.

Our first concert tour was 200 dates (Jimi Hendrix was our opening act—more about that later), and we did it all—just the four of us. No tapes, no singers or musicians backstage, not even any monitors (they hadn't been invented yet). I've often said that the Monkees becoming a real group was the equivalent of Leonard Nimoy becoming a real Vulcan. Life imitating art imitating life. I've not witnessed any thing like it until Spinal Tap.

Unfortunately, there were those who didn't see it quite this way and we often got trashed by the press. In reference to the criticism, Mike Nesmith once said, "the Monkees were like a circus where everybody just stood outside and looked at the tent. Nobody went inside."

I do think that the PTB made a mistake at the beginning of the project by not including all the various musician credits on the albums as everyone does today. And there were some great musicians playing on the tracks right from the start: Glen Campbell, Earl Palmer, Hal Blain, Buddy Miles, Billy Preston, Larry Knechtel of Bread, Harry Nilsson, Carole King, Neil Young, Stephen Stills, Hugh McCracken, and, of course, Tommy Boyce and Bobby Hart.

Not giving these guys credit gave the erroneous impression that (1) we were trying to take all the credit ourselves and (2) that we had been a group *first,* before the show. That was not only misleading, but unnecessary. I doubt if it would have made one bit of difference to our loyal fans who loved the Monkees for the freedom that we represented, for the feelings that we engendered, for the spirit that we conveyed.

Now that we were so incredibly famous, the time was rapidly approaching when we would have to "face the press."

The PTB must have been petrified. The show was a hit, the records were hits, we were feeling our oats. And we weren't used to being told what we could or couldn't talk about.

What would we say about drugs, about the war, about hippies, and love and sex and politics and religion? Peter had already made his somewhat radical leftish opinions known to anyone who would listen, and I suspect they were mostly afraid of what *he* might say, but there was some concern about all of us. We had, after all, been encouraged, nay *trained,* to be spontaneous, off the wall, irreverent, etc. etc. That worked great on the set when they had the ability to edit us in or edit us out. But what would happen with a newspaper reporter—or worse yet, a live press conference?

The president of Screen Gems, Jackie Cooper, must have thought it was his responsibility to brief us on the finer points of public relations, because one day we were all called into his office for a meeting.

Cut To:

Int. Jackie Cooper's Office—Day

The four Monkees, Jackie Cooper, Bob and Bert, and some various and sundry assistant assistants are gathered in the office.

Mike is reading a copy of *Car and Driver,* Davy is doing his nails, Micky is gazing out the window, and Peter is pacing around like a caged tiger.

JACKIE

All I'm saying is that we should be careful not to make statements that would compromise the integrity of the show and the sensibilities of the viewing audience.

PETER

Bullshit, man! That's just the same kind of bourgeoisie, establishment crap that has repressed the masses and lined the pockets of the fat-cat, big business fascist pigs!

MICKY

What?

DAVY

Does anyone have an emery board?

BOB

Peter, I sympathize with you but we discussed this, remember? And we decided that this is not the appropriate platform to expound on personal issues.

MIKE

Man, look at this new Buick Riviera. I gotta have me one of these.

Peter walks over to the window and stares out into the gray L.A. day. Bob gets up, walks over to him, and puts an arm around his shoulder. Peter starts to cry softly.

Fade Out

So we reached a compromise—we made jokes. Whenever some clever-clogs reporter tried to stir up trouble by backing us into some ideological corner, we would respond with an arsenal of witty repartee.

REPORTER: So what do you think of the war?

MICKY: What war?

REPORTER: Do you guys smoke pot?

MIKE: No, we barbecue it slowly for two hours.

REPORTER: Do you believe in free love?

DAVY: No, I always charge *something*.

REPORTER: What do you think about Nixon's foreign policy?

PETER: It's just more bourgeoisie establishment crap that . . .

ALL: PETER!

Ahhh, these were heady days, indeed. The filming of the show couldn't have been going better. I was in my element and loved every minute of it. Any successful TV show attracts guest stars and we had our share: Julie Newmar, Jerry Colonna, Stan Freberg, Rose Marie, and Hans Conried.

Jim Frawley and Bob Rafelson were doing most of the directing, but we would occasionally have a guest director. Usually, they would do one episode and we would never see them again. Directing *The Monkees* must have been the assignment from hell. It wasn't that we were offensive or ill-behaved (usually), we were just wacky, nutty, and totally uncontrollable—and that was on a good day.

One day Jerry Lewis visited the set, presumably to consider directing an episode. I for one was thrilled. I was a big fan of his—I still am. We were introduced to him and then he watched us filming for a while, running around, tearing up the set, playing practical jokes on the crew, harassing the other actors. Regrettably, he never came back.

Working on *The Monkees* wasn't tough only on the directors (two directors actually died after working on our show!), it was hell on the guest actors. They were used to working on conventional shows like *I Dream of Jeannie* and *The Flying Nun*, where "improvisation" was a dirty word. Suddenly, they found themselves right in the middle of insanity city, without cab fare.

Some dealt with the dementia well, some didn't. Rose Marie and Stan Freberg were especially good at adapting to our eccentric style, but poor Hans Conried, great actor that he was, simply couldn't cope.

He was guest starring in one particular episode (I don't remember which one, they all ran together after a while), and we were being particularly mischievous that day. The trouble with creating the kind of spontaneously combustive atmosphere that Bob and Bert had worked so hard to achieve is that it's difficult to contain. You constantly run the risk of it going critical at any moment and burning a hole through the center of the Earth. On this particular day we were pushing the limits, and well on our way to meltdown.

We'd been trying to get through this one particular scene for quite some time, but kept going off into cloud cuckoo land. The director and crew were used to this kind of thing by now, but Mr. Conried was not. Finally, after ten or twenty takes, he threw up his arms in frustration and screamed, "God I hate these fucking kids!" I've always regretted upsetting him like that. Maybe when the producers sent the actors their scripts they should have included plans for emergency evacuation.

What with working seven days a week I didn't have much of a personal life. But who needed it? Being on the set or in the recording studio all the time could hardly be considered hard labor. There were always friends around and occasionally some girls. (In my case there were usually girls around and occasionally some friends.)

My best friend at the time was still Rick Klein, the guy that I'd gone to architectural school with. I'd offered him the job of my stand-in and he had accepted. He and I formed the nucleus of my personal cabal. Each of us had a core of faithful followers, and we eventually formed our own, discrete cliques (sometimes they could have been described as warring tribes).

Each of us had his own large dressing room that we were free to furnish and decorate as we pleased. This is where we hung out, held court, conducted our business affairs, and conducted our affair affairs. I'll describe them to you (the dressing rooms, not the affairs), and you might glean something of an insight into our individual personalities:

DAVY: Classic Hollywood/Broadway. Big mirror covering one whole wall, surrounded by a hundred lightbulbs. Pictures, postcards, letters, and opening-night telegrams encircle the mirror and cover the remaining walls. The only furniture is a bunk bed and a filing cabinet—to hold more pictures, postcards, letters, and opening-night telegrams.

PETER: Wall-to-wall musical instruments and assorted paraphernalia. Keyboards, guitars, amps, microphones, tape recorders, sheet music. You never had to look around for Peter. If you needed him you could always find him hunched over his Fender Rhodes practicing a Bach Three-Part Invention.

MIKE: Country/Western/Psychedelic. Dark and foreboding. Dimly lit by a string of Christmas tree lights. Black light posters and aluminum foil covered the walls, stacks of *Car and Driver* magazines covered the coffee table. For some strange reason that I never understood, he had stuck a couple of hundred safety pins in one wall. I often wondered what went on in that dressing room.

MICKY: Extra thick shag carpet covered the floor *and* walls. Piles of paisley pillows—and a candle. (I guess that shows you where I was at.)

Yes I admit it I was girl-crazy. I still am. I have been all my life. I just love loving women. And being in my position gave me a license to steal. I was like a kid in a carnal store. I'd like to think that I wasn't too sexually aggressive (No one ever ran out of my dressing room screaming "Rape!") However, I certainly did make the best of my celebrity. (Now that I think about it, there were a couple of times that *I* ran out of my dressing room screaming "Rape!")

With Davy and I living together, there was a formidable bevy of beauties who passed through our portals (sorry, no names).

And why not? Men like beautiful women; women like successful men. That is simply the nature of the beast, and I make no apologies.

> Sex endows the individual with a dumb and powerful instinct, which carries his body and soul continually towards another; makes it one of the dearest employments of his life to select and pursue a companion, and joins to possession the keenest pleasure, to rivalry the fiercest rage, and to solitude an eternal melancholy. What more could be needed to suffuse the world with the deepest meaning and beauty?
>
> —George Santayana
> *The Sense of Beauty*

But what with everything going on at the time, there weren't actually that many opportunities to "get down" (the sixties equivalent of "party"). After coming home from a hard day's work slaving over a hot Monkeemobile, or being chased around the Columbia back lot by a bunch of extras in werewolf costumes, I was lucky if I could get up the stairs and get into bed, much less get it up. And as if I wasn't busy enough, I was soon to get even busier.

I don't know if Bob and Bert had actually counted on our really being able to play as a band or not. You'd have to ask them. But it wasn't long after the show was on the air, and the records were in the charts, that there must have been a extraordinary demand for us to appear in concert, because they came to us and we started talking about touring.

They told us they had hired this guy named David Winters, and he was going to "stage" our show. At the time, David was best known as one of the original members of the Broadway cast of *West Side Story*. Well, we weren't so sure that we needed to be staged, but we went along with it and the relationship did happen to click. David couldn't do too much about our sound or the songs we had to play, but he was very helpful in establishing the show order and directing us in our solo numbers.

Besides playing all the Monkees songs as a group, each of us was to have a solo spot in the show where we could do whatever we wanted. Peter was going to do a banjo piece; Mike worked up something by Bo Diddley; Davy was doing a Broadway tune; and I chose to do an old Ray Charles rock & roll song called "I Gotta Woman," complete with the James Brown impersonation that I'd salvaged from my days in the sharkskin suits.

The first date was booked! December 3, 1966, in Honolulu, Hawaii. (Very clever. That way, if we bombed, who would know?)

We rehearsed frantically. I played those stinking drums until my hands bled. Then I would bandage them up, put on gloves, and start again. We were busting our asses because we knew that when we got up there on the stage there wouldn't be any special effects, or camera tricks, or clever editing, or elaborate recording techniques to cover our butts. It was just going to be us, all alone.

Cut To:

Int. Monkees Dressing Room—Honolulu—Night

The Monkees are getting dressed in their new red velvet, custom-made show clothes. They have been told that the place is packed. They are nervous as hell. The dressing room is a beehive of activity. Bob Rafelson is there giving last minute support, David Winters is there giving last minute instructions, roadies are running in and out carrying messages to and from the hinterland that is the waiting stage.

MICKY

Shit! Where are my drumsticks?

Instantly, an assistant assistant scrambles into action and Micky's drumsticks appear in his hand almost before he finishes speaking.

DAVY

Hey, guys? Which eyeliner do you like better?

PETER

Fuck the eyeliner. Where are my finger picks?

Bam! They appear in his hand as if out of thin air.

MIKE
(slow drawl)

Come on, guys. Take it easy. There's only twenty *thousand* people out there to see us.

The dressing room door opens and Bert Schneider comes in.

BERT
(solemnly)

It's time.

A hush falls over the room. In the distance we can hear a low, throbbing rumble.

MICKY

Shit! What's that?

MIKE

Come on, guys. Let's go.

With that they file out of the room led by all the PTB, and followed closely by all the PTWB (powers that wannabe).

They work their way through the underground maze of the concert hall and scramble up the ramp onto the back of the stage.

Cut To:

Int. Concert Hall—Night

The auditorium is dark. The massive, squirming crowd looks like a living, moving sea of one-celled organisms. On stage, you can barely see the outlines of the rock & roll equipment. On each side of the stage is a large black box that looks like a giant amplifier. The word "VOX" is painted on the front of each box.

Suddenly, an announcer's voice comes over the PA system.

ANNOUNCER (V.O.)

And now, ladies and gentlemen, KPOI radio is proud to present . . . THE M.......

He never gets to finish. He's drowned out by a Promethean roar.

Suddenly, a huge movie screen (the first ever to be used on the road) ignites with the image of *The Monkees* opening television sequence. Simultaneously, THE MONKEES THEME SONG comes blasting out over the massive sound system.

Cut To:

Int. Vox Box—Night

The boxes aren't amplifiers at all. Micky and Davy are tucked inside one of the huge set pieces, ready to come bursting out. (Peter and Mike are in the other one.) When they hear the crowd roar they exchange looks of wonder, surprise, and abject terror.

Cut To:

Int. Concert Hall—Night

As the crowd writhes hysterically, two follow-spots light up the front of the VOX boxes. The crowd surges forward.

Cut To:

Int. Vox Box—Night

On cue, Micky and Davy brace themselves and erupt out of the box and onto the stage. Micky has rehearsed this before, but nothing can prepare him for what he encounters.

Cut To:

Int. Concert Hall—Night

The scream of the crowd reaches an inconceivable decibel. (It is reported later that the noise is heard as far away as the Philippines.) Then, as if on cue, twenty thousand little Kodak Instamatic flash cubes go off at exactly the same time. Micky is blinded and stumbles around, trying to find his way to the drum set.

He finally makes his way to the drum riser and saddles up. The THEME SONG finishes. The stage lights up with color. He looks at Mike and gets an affirmative nod. Mike turns to the crowd and breaks into the opening lick of "The Last Train to Clarksville."

The crowd goes bananas.

Fade Out

We pulled it off. Actually, we not only pulled it off, we were pretty good. Not that it would have mattered much what we sounded like; the audience screamed for the entire hour and a half. I for one couldn't hear a thing. I played that concert more by sight than by sound.

That was a special night for me. I'll never forget that feeling when I popped out of that silly box and ran into that wall of sound and light. It was also very special because later that night, when we were driving back to the hotel in the limousine, I noticed there was a stranger in the front seat. It was a woman. I asked, "Who's that?" She turned around. It was my mom.

That night was to open a whole new world for me. The world of the rock & roll megatour. A tour that would eventually take me all over the States, all over the world. I would go everywhere from Tokyo to Tucson, meet everyone from Brenda Lee to the Beatles; get high, get low, get laid, get rich, get ripped off, and get married.

Things just never were the same after that.

Seven

The Long
and
Whining
Road

You have ravished me away by a power I cannot

resist; and yet I could resist till I saw you;

and even since I have seen you I have

endeavored often "to reason against

the reason of my Love."

—John Keats
Letter to Fanny Brawne

Our first proper tour started in Denver, Colorado, on the day after Christmas 1966. I won't bore you with the various times and places of the other concerts, you can look them up in any number of Monkeethologies. (I would have to look them up myself, anyway.) We played half-a-dozen dates or so, and this little "test" tour ended on December 31 in Nashville, Tennessee, where we celebrated the incoming year at Brenda Lee's New Year's Eve party.

One of the dates on that tour was in San Francisco, at the Cow Palace. That date sticks out in my mind because that was the first time my whole family had seen me perform as a Monkee. They drove up from San Jose to attend the concert. I can only imagine what it must have been like for them to see me on stage in that huge arena, amidst the glaring lights, the screaming multitudes, the relentless cacophony.

The effects that stardom can have on an individual are often two-faced. Fame and notoriety are balanced by the demise of any personal privacy. The reverence of adoring fans is tempered by the vindictiveness of jealous wannabes. The pleasures enjoyed by having embarrassingly large amounts of money becomes inversely proportional to the aggravation and litigation that always seem to follow. The effects that exceptional celebrity can have on the luminary's family can be just as dualistic.

I'm sure that all my sisters were very proud of me, but I'm also sure that, at times, they had deeply wished that the Monkees would just go away and Micky would come home. I know for a fact that at one time or the other they all went through an "I hate the Monkees" stage. And who could blame them? When word got out who their sibling was, they were either brown-nosed by insincere opportunists or jeered at by covetous fools.

My sister Coco often complained that she never knew if her friends were really being her friends or if they were just being friendly so they could eventually get close to me. My sister Debbie broke down in tears one day as she told me about her years of torment being known at school as "Monkee Girl."

The stories of families being torn asunder by the extraordinary success of one of its members are legend. Coco calls it "living in the shadow." I think it's a credit to my mother, to my sisters, and to our stepfather, Dr. Robert Scott, that there was so *little* damage done. You only have to read about other show-biz families, past and present, to appreciate that it could have been a lot worse.

I didn't see a lot of my family during those months. But the Monkees phenomenon touched them all in one way or another. I had the bright idea one day of making my grandmother, Mamoo, the president of my fan club. She ran that club like clockwork for many years—until her death. She was loved and revered by thousands of my fans.

My mom also got intimately involved with the Monkees, though I'm afraid it wasn't so much by choice as by necessity.

Since *The Monkees* was initially a TV show, and I was hired as an actor to play the part of a drummer, I was paid accordingly. My starting salary was $450 a week! That increased somewhat over the years to come, but certainly wasn't a patch on the astronomical salaries that TV stars take home these days. But there *were* ancillary benefits . . .

One day, Lester Sill, who had become the president of Colgems Records, our *personal* recording company, met with me for lunch. During the course of the meal, he reached into his pocket, pulled out an envelope, and handed it to me.

"Congratulations," he said.

I opened the envelope, took out the check, counted the zeros, counted them again, and, after picking myself up off the floor, said, "Shit, what am I going to do with this?"

At the time, I had no professional representation. Bob, Bert, and Ward Sylvester, the associate producer on the show had (cleverly) talked me into breaking my contract with my agent. Actually, none of us had outside agents or managers. That way, there would be no one to come between our producers and their creations. One day, in that great old Hollywood tradition, they put their collective arms around my innocent shoulders and said, through toothy smiles, "Don't worry kid. We'll take care of you." (Naughty, naughty, B&B.)

So I didn't have anybody close at hand who could tell me what to do with this little rectangular piece of paper with the big dollar sign followed by a telephone number. That was, actually, quite fortunate for me. I'm afraid that some of the other guys weren't as lucky. Davy, in particular, was more than once victimized by swindlers, brigands, and thieves. (I'm sure that these unfortunate experiences contributed to the self-sabotaging pathology that was to become such an obstacle to our mutual success in the future—more about that later.)

Davy was not stupid, he was just vulnerable. He simply

didn't have anyone around he could really trust. He didn't even have anyone around he could trust enough to ask *who* to trust. Neither did I, but fortunately, before some highwayman had a chance to ambush my stagecoach and plunder my riches, I called the only person in the world I knew I *could* trust, my mom.

Poor Mom. Here she was, living a nice quiet life in the foothills of the Santa Cruz mountains, bringing up three lovely little daughters, watching her son the pop star take the world by storm, when one day she gets a call from said pop star son. He tells her about the bit of paper with all the zeros on it, and after she picks herself up off the floor, they decide that the best and safest thing to do is to have her look after the money for a while, for only a "little" while, until things settle down and proper arrangements can be made. Well things never did settle down, and my mom looked after my affairs for years—brilliantly.

Unfortunately, this did cause some internal problems within the family. The girls felt, justifiably, that they were not getting their fair share of her time and attention. Of course, these days working mothers have become the norm instead of the exception, and I can only thank them, and her, for the sacrifices they made on my behalf.

Meanwhile, back in Monkeeland . . .

If I hadn't been totally jazzed before the tour, I certainly was now. My head must have swelled up as large as my bass drum. The frenzy that had been Honolulu followed us everywhere we went. There was no denying it . . . We were big! I took limos everywhere and was constantly followed by a entourage of fawning yes-men and swarming press-men. I was on the cover of every teen-scene magazine on the supermarket shelf, and under the covers with every lean/teen/beauty queen I could find. I was hustled here and hustled there, in and out of hotels, airports, radio stations, TV stations, and concert halls. More than once I found myself in the back of an ice-cream truck or a meat wagon being surreptitiously spirited into or out of a concert hall lest I be dismembered by a flock of frenzied females. (I just *love* alliteration.)

Simultaneously, Columbia/Screen Gems, who owned the name "The Monkees," started marketing the name, the logo, and our likenesses in every way they possibly could. Overnight there was Monkee merchandise available everywhere: Monkee dolls, lunch boxes, games, puzzles, books, posters, cars, cards, puppets, calendars, cups, rings, things . . . You name it, I was on it. But, believe it or not, I never saw a cent from this marketing bonanza. Somehow the "merchandising" clause of my contract had been mysteriously omitted. When I brought this to Bob and Bert's attention I, once again, felt their collective arms slither around my shoulders: "Don't worry, kid. There's enough to go around. We'll work something out." (Naughty, naughty B&B.)

Don't get me wrong, I did *very* well out of *The Monkees*, and I am grateful. I'm still getting jobs today based on the success and prestige I accrued by my association with that project. But it would have been nice to get a fair deal. And, quite simply, I didn't.

But, onward and upward.

Our new single, "I'm a Believer," was released. It was written by this new singer/songwriter named Neil Diamond. On the back was "Steppin' Stone" by Boyce and Hart. I sang the lead on both songs. "Believer" was number one for seven weeks, "Steppin' Stone" charted at number twenty. The first album, *The Monkees*, had sold millions of copies, and the second album, *More of the Monkees*, was destined to sell zillions, holding the number-one spot in *Billboard* for eighteen weeks.

Between me, Mike, Davy, Peter, Tommy Boyce and Bobby Hart, Bob and Bert, Carole King, Neil Diamond, Lester Sill, Donnie Kirshner, and the host of other writers, producers, promoters, sponsors, associates, executives, underlings, and overlings associated with the enterprise, we had broken all the existing pop-chart records and even eclipsed those held by the Beatles and the Rolling Stones. Not bad for the sixties' version of Spinal Tap.

I was very proud of my participation in all this. I still am. And to all of those who criticized, condemned, berated, lambasted, denounced, defamed, defiled, or otherwise desecrated the Monkees . . . Go fuck yourselves.

But despite all of the success, all of the adulation, that little seedling of musical discontent had finally taken root and was growing up big and strong. It was now a healthy sapling, its leaves unfolding, its roots extending deep into the ground of Monkeeland; the sapling was starting to sap the life out of the group.

With Mike holding our banner high, we were all starting to talk about things like "creative control" and "active participation." Mike and Peter had even put their differences aside and had formed an uneasy alliance (kind of like the USA and Russia during the Gulf War). They perceived the executives at RCA and at Screen Gems Music as the common enemy, and everything that was wrong with the picture, all the Machiavellian manipulation, was personified in one man . . . Donnie Kirshner.

To be honest, I remember very little about Donnie Kirshner. In years to come he was to claim the title of "Monkeemaker." That was certainly an overestimation, but he undoubtedly had a profound influence on what we recorded and what was released and, hence, our musical careers.

At the time, all I knew was that he worked out of New York and was being called the "music director." The first time I met him was in a recording studio in L.A. We were recording some track or another and here was this guy in a suit who showed up and stood around, occasionally throwing in his two cents' worth. It was getting more difficult to "contain" the four of us at the best of times, let alone when things weren't going so well, or when it was late at night, or when we were just in that "crazy kind of guys" mood. At those times, we could be absolutely intolerable. This was one of those times.

The session was running late and, for some reason, the producers couldn't get a good sound on the bass. I was getting impatient, I had places to go, things to see, people to do. Suddenly, this guy in a suit, this stranger from New York, says something inane about "putting some high EQ on the low end." I had just finished a cup of Coca-Cola and the cup was still full of ice. I figured it was about time for a laugh, so I casually turned the cup upside down on Donnie's head. The ice stayed there for a moment like an inverted snow cone. It worked. Everyone laughed. Except Donnie. He had a quiet word with me later and I agreed not to humiliate him again if he would agree not to bitch about the bass sound.

But Mr. Kirshner must have had a lot of power, or else somebody was making him the scapegoat, because he was the one Mike would often refer to as the "opposition."

I don't want to make Mike out as a troublemaker. It was simply a case of seeing the picture from a different perspective. Mike was determined to wrest the "creative control" of the music from the PTB, and they were determined to hold it firmly within their hot little wealthy hands. From their point of view they must have thought, "His records are selling like Hula Hoops. What the hell does this guy want?" Of course that was the problem. They weren't *his* records. If anything, they were *my* records, or *Davy's* records. Mike was lucky to get a couple of songs on each album, but his songs were never picked as the singles. I don't think it was a case of jealousy, but here he was, raking in the dough, basking in the fame, and he must have felt that he hadn't done a lot to deserve it. To his way of thinking, it must have felt very illegitimate.

I was torn. On the one hand, I was very happy with the way the sessions were going, and I certainly couldn't fault the results. I could sense that the creative decisions being made were the right ones for the project, and those feelings were confirmed by the extraordinary record sales. On the other hand, I had a very intense, personal relationship with Mike and the other guys. I couldn't just divorce myself from the issue and pretend it didn't exist. Because of my quandary I tried desperately to keep in the middle, not rock the boat. After all, the "boat" was a bloody gold-plated battleship. I got called "wishy-washy" for my efforts. But it just kept getting worse and worse. The PTB were continuing to control the recording/releasing mechanisms, Mike was digging in his heels, and we continued to acquire more power and influence. The sapling had become a very large tree that cast its shadow over all of Monkeedom.

Ironically, I was more upset over the fab/gear clothes we were forced to wear on the cover of *More of the Monkees*. The PTB had made some kind of sponsorship deal with JCPenney, and we had got stuck wearing these hideous outfits. (Sorry JCPenney, but they *were* awful.)

At the end of January 1967, everything came to a head. We had been invited to Donnie Kirshner's suite at the Beverly Hills Hotel to be given our Gold albums for *More of the Monkees*.

Cut To:

Int. Kirshner's Bungalow—Night

The four Monkees, Donnie Kirshner, and Herb Moelis (a Screen Gems lawyer) are in attendance. The boys have just arrived and pleasantries have been exchanged. The atmosphere is tense. Everyone knows what's coming, and no one is looking forward to it.

Micky is lounging in a chair, dreading the inevitable. Peter is standing against a wall with his arms folded. Davy is doing his nails. This time it's Mike who's pacing like a caged tiger.

Donnie has four Gold records stacked up on a table. He

picks them up and hands them to the guys. He grins a big toothy grin.

DONNIE

So, here they are guys. You're sparkling new Gold records! Congratulations!

MICKY
(feigned enthusiasm)

Great!

DAVY
(feigned enthusiasm)

Great!

PETER
(no enthusiasm)

Hummph!

MIKE
(ominously)

When is the next release scheduled?

DONNIE
(cautiously)

Well . . . we think it should be in late February . . . or so.

PETER
(sarcastically)

Well, guys. I guess we'd better get into the studio and start recording some new tunes. *Our* tunes.

Donnie's big toothy grin starts to fade. All you can see now are the tips of the fangs.

DONNIE

No, no. Don't bother. We've already recorded some great new tracks in New York. There's this one unbelievable tune by Neil Diamond . . . You remember him, he wrote "I'm a Bel . . ."

MIKE
(exploding)

What! You recorded new tracks in New York? Why the hell didn't you talk to us first? It's our names going on those records!

Whatever was left of the big toothy smile is gone and lost forever. It has been replaced by a thin, grim smirk.

DONNIE

Take it easy, kid. Why don't you just be happy with this Gold record and . . .

MIKE

Look! Either we get total and complete control of all the recording *and* the releases or I'm quitting!

Donnie is taken aback; the grim grin is frozen on his face. Even the other three guys are stunned. No one thought it would come to this. And no one thinks for a moment that Mike is bluffing. Mike doesn't bluff. Suddenly, Herb Moelis, the *lawyer* speaks up.

MOELIS
(arrogantly)

You'd better take look at your contract, *son*. You can't quit unless we *tell* you you can quit.

Big mistake! This is not something you tell Mike Nesmith, even as a joke, on a *good* day. Mike spins around to confront the squirmy legal beagle. There is fire in his eyes and fury in his heart. His fists are clenched. The veins are popping out of his neck. He looks like he is about to explode all over this little litigator. Somehow he manages to maintain his self-control.

He turns to the nearby wall, cocks back his fist, and plunges it deep into the thirty-year-old lath and plaster.

MIKE

THAT COULD HAVE BEEN YOUR FACE, MOTHER-FUCKER!

With that he storms out of the seething room and into the cool L.A. night.

Fade Out

Because of Mike's ultimatum, the PTB were in quite a quandary. Who should they replace, the group's musical director, or one of the members of the group?

I was still reeling. I'd had no idea that the issue had become so critical. The whole battle between Mike, Donnie, and the PTB must have been going on for quite some time, and, to this day, I don't know what transpired between Mike and the PTB behind closed doors.

The next thing I knew was that we had a new record producer, Chip Douglas. Mike had found him playing bass with the Turtles at the Whiskey-A-Go-Go and, after consulting the rest of us, asked him if he wanted to take on the Monkees. He said yes.

In an effort to make everybody happy, Bert Schneider agreed to let the Monkees have 50 percent input on the material from that point on. Kirshner reluctantly agreed. In other words, the next single had to have a homegrown Monkees song on the B side.

Chip and Mike immediately went into the recording studio and recut one of Mike's compositions that was left over from one of our first recording sessions. The song was "The Girl I Knew Somewhere." But when it was presented to Kirshner, he refused to release it as the B side of our third single.

Now, you may be wondering why it was so important for Mike to have his song on the B side of our next single release. Well, aside from the obvious desire to have his music, his art, and his voice heard on record, the fact of the matter is that publishing companies don't make a distinction between who writes what on which side of a hit record. The writer of the B side gets the same royalty as the writer of the A side, even if the B side never gets played. With our singles selling in the multimillions, this added up to quite a tidy sum! Mike Nesmith was no fool.

Meanwhile, Davy was instructed to go into the studio and record the lead vocal for "A Little Bit Me, a Little Bit You," and Don Kirshner authorized the release of the song as a single, backed with another one of the songs from his stable of writers: Jeff Barry's "She Hangs Out." Kirshner must have thought he had won the battle, but, because of that move, he lost the war.

To make a long (and somewhat boring) story short, Kirshner was eventually fired as our "musical director," Boyce and Hart were out as producers, and Chip Douglas was installed as our *new* producer. The single "A Little Bit, etc." backed with "She Hangs Out" was pulled off the market and immediately replaced with "A Little Bit, etc." on the A side and Mike's tune on the other. This set the stage for our third album, *Headquarters,* which would become a landmark in our careers in that at least 50 percent of the material would be supplied by us (or Chip Douglas) and, as far as the music went, we would play every fucking note.

I was just rolling with the punches. For better or for worse I had put all my eggs in Mike's basket and was happy to let the cards fall where they may. As a sign of solidarity, I had refused to show up at a Kirshner-sponsored recording session in New York and, instead, hopped on board a plane for England where I was due to start a press junket. While the battle for creative control was raging on both coasts of the colonies, I took up residence at the stately Grovesnor House hotel, Park Lane, London.

As if all this wasn't bad enough, back in L.A., Mike had called a press conference. In front of reporters from *Look* and *Time* magazine, he let the Monkee out of the bag. He revealed that much of the tracking work on the first two albums had been done by studio musicians.

Simultaneously, I was confronted by reporters in England who were asking the same questions. When asked if we had played all the music on the albums I innocently said, "No, but we never said we did."

Well, the feces really slammed into the proverbial whirling blades. The press, who up until then had loved us, turned and crucified us. I was dazed. Suddenly, the reality of the situation hit me. "Shit! These people actually think we were born into this band. They really think we all live together in this funky beach house and Davy's eyes really do sparkle when he sees a girl, and the stuffed chimpanzee in the corner really does talk. They really think Leonard Nimoy *is* a Vulcan!"

I had been very naive. It was obvious that these people took their rock & roll very seriously. I tried to explain about *The Monkees* being a show *about* a group, but it fell on deaf ears. They felt they had been used and misused, bamboozled, hoodwinked, and deceived.

Looking back now, there's no question in my mind that we were terribly exploited and manipulated by the PTB. They could have easily set us up in an honest, straightforward situation. They must have known what was eventually going to happen. If they were going to screw us, at least they could have used protection. Instead, they followed their bank balances instead of their hearts. I felt like an innocent bystander caught in the middle of a war zone, getting blown to bits, while the generals were sitting back in command central courting their chicks and cashing their checks (Naughty, naughty, naughty, B&B.)

Ironically, it didn't seem to make one bit of difference to our fans. I'd venture to say it never has. I don't remember receiving one negative fan letter or hearing one negative comment from a fan about the use of other musicians. It seems that they knew, intuitively, what was going on right from the start and were always way ahead of the press (which isn't hard).

Despite all this negative hoopla, I was having a great time in London. The English gutter press had failed to even make a dent in the popularity of the Monkees and I was the talk of the town. I was treated like a visiting dignitary, and the biggest day of my life came when I was invited to meet Paul McCartney!

As I drove through St. John's Wood on my way to his house, I reminisced how, just months before, I had been driving down Ventura Boulevard, listening to Beatle tunes, and here I was, about to meet my idol! And what's more, I was meeting him, not as a fan, but as a peer! I knew I had to stay cool, but I also knew that it would take all the self-control I could muster not to ask him for his autograph.

Cut To:

Int. Paul's House—Day

Micky is ushered into the house by Paul's press secretary. A photographer is present to capture this historical moment when "Monkee meets Beatle."

Micky is extremely nervous on the inside, but managing to keep his external cool. He checks his back pocket to make sure the autograph book is still there . . . just in case.

Paul appears in the hallway. He is cool, confident, friendly, disarming.

PAUL

Hello.

MICKY

Hi.

PAUL

Want a smoke?

Micky knows he isn't talking about cigarettes.

MICKY
(relieved)

I thought you'd never ask.

Paul rolls an enormous joint of hash and tobacco and lights it up. The sweet, pungent smell of the high-quality herb fills the room. The atmosphere is quiet, classical, eternal. At any moment Micky expects to see Oscar Wilde walk in from the kitchen, sit down, and take a puff.

The photographer discreetly snaps a few shots of Paul and Micky sitting around; Paul discreetly holds the joint like a cigarette. Curiously, Paul turns on the television.

PAUL
(mischievously)

Take a look at what's on TV.

Under any other circumstances, Micky would have thought it very strange for someone to turn on a TV at a time like this, but something tells him it's okay. Actually, Paul could have suggested that they glue their tongues to the ceiling and Micky would have thought that was okay too.

The photographer and press person slide out of the room, and Paul turns the TV to a spare channel. Typical TV snow fills the screen. He fiddles with the contrast for a moment, turns down the sound of the white noise, and sits back in the couch. Micky watches the blank screen for a moment.

MICKY

I don't get it.

PAUL

Just watch.

Micky watches. Suddenly, all the little white dots start to coalesce. They seem to be forming images! Micky peers more closely. It's true. Out of the seemingly random pattern of dancing dots, visions are appearing. First it's a dancing girl, then a landscape, then a face. It's constantly changing, morphing from one illusory apparition to another.

Micky takes another hit on the monster joint. He looks at it, then back at the TV. Which is it that's creating the effect? The TV or the joint? Who cares?

MICKY

Far out.

PAUL

Hmmm . . .

Fade Out

It took me a while to figure out that it was, indeed, the television that created the fantasmagoric illusions and not the hemp. We were actually watching some spurious signals that were bleeding over from other channels. Try it sometime. It's neat. (The television trick, not the hemp.)

The next day I got the thrill of a lifetime. Paul invited me to a Beatle recording session! I was overjoyed. I was elated. I was euphoric. What would I wear?

What would it be like? A dark, smoke-filled, psychedelic cavern? Cluttered with exotic, state-of-the-art recording equipment? Peopled by exotic, state-of-the-era musical illuminants and their naked nubile nymphs? (I *love* alliteration.)

The next morning I was picked up by the limo and driven to the EMI recording studios on Abbey Road. (Yes, over that *very* crosswalk.) I was ushered into the building and down a long flight of stairs into the studio. I braced myself for what I did not know.

It looked like a hospital! Bright, fluorescent lights, sterile, pale walls of some indistinguishable color. Amps and instruments placed strategically around the room. And the Fab Four sat in straight-backed chairs working diligently on some track. (Sorry, I was so dizzy from the experience that to this day I'll be damned if I can remember what tune they were working on.)

Shortly after I arrived they decided to have a "cuppa." They put down their instruments, and a quiet gentleman's gentleman brought down a tray full of teacups and a teapot. We sat at a small card table, drank tea, and chatted for about twenty minutes. Then, like the responsible working-class lads that they were, someone noted the time, someone else clapped his hands, Ringo said, "Right, back to it lads," and they went back down into the pits.

Meanwhile, the press were making a big deal out of the imaginary Monkee/Beatle battle, and it was around this time that

John Lennon made the Monkee/Marx Brothers comparison. I was so glad that he did. It was extremely embarrassing to be compared to the Beatles. That wasn't what the Monkees was about. To use the *Star Trek* analogy again, it would have been like comparing William Shatner to Neil Armstrong.

Mike Nesmith arrived in London soon after and, together, we started making the publicity rounds. One of the stops was the BBC, where we were to make a surprise appearance on the biggest pop show of the time, arguably of *all* time, *Top of the Pops*.

Somehow, word had gotten out that we were going to appear on the show, so they had to smuggle us into the complex in the trunk of a Daimler limousine. Inside, we were on our way to the stage when we passed by the studio cafeteria. I happened to glance inside, and it was lucky that I did. That glance changed my life.

My personal life at that point had been pretty nonexistent. It was impossible to have a steady girlfriend at the time (not that I wanted one), but I was also getting fed up with the endless procession of faceless, nameless people who were drifting in and out of my life. Being the healthy red-blooded American/Indian/Italian boy that I was, I was always quick to appreciate an example of the fine feminine form, but nothing I had experienced had prepared me for what was about to happen.

Cut To:

Int. BBC Studios—Day

Micky is being hustled down a gray-green hall by his British adjunct. As he passes the studio cafeteria he glances inside and his eye catches the most unbelievable sight. There, framed in the doorway, is a vision. She is tall, blond, beautiful, and wearing an emerald green outfit that ends up in a short skirt (very short), which tops off her unbelievably gorgeous legs.

As he passes by she looks up. Their eyes meet. She holds his glance briefly then looks away quickly with that haughty sophistication that only the British can do so well.

Micky grabs his adjunct by the arm.

MICKY

Who the fuck was that?

ADJUNCT

Oh, that was Samantha Juste. She's the cohost of the show. Do you want to meet her?

MICKY
(sarcastically)

Meet her? No, I want to have her bronzed.

Micky is a basket case after that. He and Mike are introduced on the show to a hysterical crowd, the host of the show, Jimmy Savile, asks them questions, they answer, the crowd screams every time they open their mouths, but Micky is in another world. He just keeps watching the girl in the green dress as she plays a record, smiles, flirts with the audience, and dances.

After the show, as they are hustled out of the building and back into the trunk of the limo, the adjunct notices that Micky is looking around frantically.

ADJUNCT
(smiling conspiratorially)

Do you want me to get in touch with her for you?

MICKY
(leering stupidly)

What a dumb question.

Fade Out

That night, under the pretense of a "record company promotion," she was invited up to the hotel. When she showed up there was just me, my adjunct, and a bottle of champagne—the adjunct left. (God am I bad!) We talked for hours. We talked for days. We talked for nights.

I hadn't realized it at the time but she was quite a celebrity in her own right. When the press got wind of our romance, they splashed the story and our pictures across every paper in the country: "SAMANTHA TRAPS MONKEE"; "POPS GIRL GOES APE," etc. (Don't you just *love* the gutter press?)

We fell deeply, madly, and completely in love. And poor Samantha was beaten up pretty badly for her trouble (figuratively speaking). The fans instantly hated her for taking me off the market, and everywhere we went she was met with jeers and jibes. She even showed up one day with ink stains on the emerald green dress, courtesy of a resentful fan.

But nothing, or nobody, stood a chance of quelling our passion. We were inseparable. We finally managed to avoid all the unwanted attention by holing up in her trendy London flat. We stocked up on provisions, took the phone off the hook, turned on the TV, and didn't leave that place for a week.

A Box by Any Other Name

There is no need to run outside

For better seeing, . . .

. . . Rather abide

At the center of your being;

For the more you leave it, the less you learn,

Search your heart and see . . .

The way to do is to be.

—Lao-Tzu

The English promotional tour came to an end, and reluctantly I bid fond adieu to the emerald-colored British isle and the girl in the emerald dress. I returned to L.A., where I started filming the series once again, and in March we sequestered ourselves in the studio to record *Headquarters*—the "real" Monkees debut album. Mike and Peter's dream had come true. We had become a real live group. Life had imitated art imitating life. Leonard Nimoy had become a Vulcan!

I had a fantastic time recording that album. It reminded me of the days on the road with Micky and the One-Nighters. We lived, played, argued, laughed, ate, drank, and slept in tiny studio C in the RCA building on Sunset Boulevard. We, like, really *bonded*. I mean, like, *totally*. And, as I said, we played it all.

Everything but one French horn part and a cello line. And we made *damn* sure that the musicians got their due credits. *Big* credits!

But it was also tough recording that album, especially for me. I was really having to stretch myself as a drummer (I'd only been playing for a year or so). There were constant "discussions" about all that "groove" and "feel" stuff, especially between Mike and Peter who were like two alpha elks staking out their territory by pissing on the trees.

But I was getting into the spirit of it also. I had begun to blossom as a musician myself, and I started having my own ideas about where we should be "at."

Mike had encouraged me all along to write some songs, and it was on *Headquarters* that I had my first tune recorded by the group. It was called "Randy Scouse Git," and it was all about my experiences in England: The Beatles, Samantha, the parties, the chemicals . . . everything. It even has a reference to Mama Cass who was in London at the same time. The title of the song came from some slang I'd heard on a famous British TV show called, *Till Death Do Us Part,* which was the original version of *All in the Family.* Unfortunately, the direct translation of those slang words is "horny, Liverpudlian jerk," and the British PTB insisted that I come up with an alternate title for their version of the album. So I did . . . "Alternate Title."

Even with all the healthy infighting, I still think *Headquarters* was the best album we ever did as a group. (Probably because it's the *only* album that we really ever did as a group.) Ironically, after the recording and subsequent release of *Headquarters* we never went back into the studio as just a foursome again. Now that Mike had led us in our palace revolt and we had managed to triumph over the Evil Empire, we were free to do just about anything we wanted. Remember what I said about "singularity of vision"? Well, after *Headquarters* we all enjoyed having the control of the vision so much that we didn't want to give it up to *anyone,* not even each other.

The Monkees were transmutating yet again. Whereas we had started out as four single-celled organisms at the mercy of our environment, we had gathered our forces, formed a chrysalis, and emerged as "Monkeemoth," ready to take on the world. Now that the creature had proved it could actually fly and spit fire, it went through one final mitotic permutation: splitting into four separate but related beings, still connected to the whole but acting as free agents. From then on we would still exercise our control, but we would write, produce, and record our records virtually independent of each other. In a way, we had devolved back to being the four solo artists that we had started out as, each with his own agenda, recording under the banner of the Monkees. Curiouser and curiouser.

Mike, Davy, and I were quite happy to go off in this independent direction. I'm sure that this is what Mike had had in mind all along, but poor Peter was heartbroken. All along, Peter had been waiting for this moment when we would all be in the studio together, for this divine melodic bonding, for the four of us to have a meeting of our musical minds, to have our spiritual voices sing in glorious four-part harmony. To Peter, the *Headquarters* experience was our coming of age, our rite of passage. Peter, kind soul that he is, would have loved it if we all really *had* lived in that eclectic beach house and really *were* out-of-work musicians struggling to survive in a capitalistic, bourgeoisie-pig-infested society. (Peter should probably write a book entitled *The Angst of Art*.)

But it was not to be. *Headquarters* was the first and last time that the four of us would cloister ourselves away and produce an album entirely on our own. I suppose the prevailing attitude was, "Well, we've done this recording as a group thing. Now what?" We didn't know it then, but this decision would eventually have profound repercussions.

But thoughts of profound repercussions weren't on anybody's mind in the spring of '67. *Headquarters* bolted up the charts to number one, but was displaced quickly by *Sgt. Pepper*.

(What company to be in!) The sales weren't nearly as good as our previous releases but . . . so what! It was our baby and we loved it. The PTB must have been going out of their tiny little minds. "What do those idiots think they're doing!? We could be selling *millions* more albums!" The truth was, we simply didn't give a shit. This was our art!

We continued to film more episodes of the TV show and go out on more and more isolated concert dates, with opening acts like the Fifth Dimension and Ike and Tina Turner. Ike and Tina opened for us at the Hollywood Bowl, where I made my infamous jump into the pool of water that lies between the stage and the audience. I remember being in midair over the little manmade lagoon when I realized that I still had the microphone in my hand! I threw it clear just as I hit the water. *That* would have made a headline: "MONKEE MEETS MAKER AT THE BOWL."

I'd bought a house in the Hollywood Hills and had set up shop, literally. My first major investment was a completely out-fitted machine shop: drill press, metal lathe, band saw, hand tools, every Sears Craftsman gizmo that money could buy. If I wasn't filming, or recording, or touring, you could be sure to find me ensconced in my little workshop, cutting or drilling or welding or fitting or screwing something up, or down.

I guess I'd inherited this "building" gene from my father. He had also been very good with his hands. I just loved to make things; I still do. And my greatest accomplishment was a full-size gyrocopter that I built in the den of that house in the Hollywood Hills. (And yes, I was able to get it out.) But I digress.

I went back to England to visit Samantha for a while, then I brought her over to the States for a while, and then it was back to England for more Samantha and more harassment from the yellow journalists. Somewhere along the way the Beatles threw us a big party at the famous Speakeasy nightclub in London. Everybody who was anybody was there. I was there also (I think). Anyway, I'm told I had a good time. All I remember is a small room stuffed to the rafters with outrageous pop icons, sultry pop iconettes, all the food and drink we could consume, and these little purple pills consisting of compressed rye bread mold.

In June, we all attended the Emmy Awards. *The Monkees* was up for Outstanding Comedy Series of the year. We won it. Bob and Bert got the statues (and rightly so). But that was a very proud moment for me. Television had been my life, and winning that award was the greatest compliment I could have ever received.

This was the beginning of the Summer of Love. There were love-ins, laugh-ins, and be-ins, and in the middle of June, there was only one place to be: the Monterey Pop Festival.

The festival was to be *the* social, musical, spiritual, chemical, event of the year. What should I wear? In those days, it was still politically okay to wear the skins of dead animals, so I went to a famous dead animal skin fabricator and had an Indian-style suit custom made out of antelope hide, complete with bell-bottoms and a loincloth. *Très chic.* In addition, the costume designer at the studio, a wonderful man named Gene Ashman, gave me this incredible Indian headdress from the wardrobe department. I was stylin'!

Peter and I arrived in Monterey, worked our way to the County Fair Grounds where the festival was to be held, ingested some rye bread mold, and started to mix in with the in crowd: Janis Joplin, the Mamas and the Papas, the Who, Ravi Shankar, Jefferson Airplane, Otis Redding, the Animals, and the Jimi Hendrix Experience.

The first time I'd seen Hendrix was in New York at some club in the Village. He was playing lead guitar for the John Hammond band. I'd been invited down to hear "this guy play with his teeth." Sure enough, there was this young black guy who, besides being an extraordinary guitar picker, would occasionally raise the instrument up to his mouth and play it with his teeth.

Jimi must have left the States shortly after that and gone to

England, because when I saw him at Monterey he had already picked up Mitch Mitchell and Noel Redding and they had formed the Experience. I remember sitting in the audience with Peter when they came on stage. "Hey, that's the guy that plays guitar with his teeth!" I exclaimed. Not only that, but he had graduated to setting it on fire as well. On the last night of the festival, after all of the concerts, after all of the special events, after all of the fans and reporters had left, the place was still buzzing with activity. The hard-core music lovers didn't want to leave. I spent the entire night in one of the empty livestock barns listening to Jimi Hendrix jam the night away.

It just so happened that we were due to begin our summer tour in a couple of weeks, and we still needed another opening act. When I got back to L.A. I mentioned Hendrix and his impressive theatrics to Bob and Bert. The Monkees was very theatrical in my eyes and so was the Jimi Hendrix Experience. It would make the perfect union. Jimi must have thought so too, because a few weeks later he agreed to be the opening act for our upcoming summer tour.

Before we left for the tour, we went into the recording studio with Chip Douglas and recorded our fourth album, *Pisces, Aquarius, Capricorn & Jones Ltd.* It was on this album that we each started to flourish as singer/songwriter/producers. I started writing more, thanks to Mike's perpetual encourage-ment, and getting more songs on the albums. Again, we made sure that all the musicians we used to supplement the tracks were given full credit. It was on this album that I sang what I think is one of the best tunes we ever did, "Pleasant Valley Sunday" by Carole King and Gerry Goffin.

One day on the set, I was told that some guy wanted to meet me about some new musical instrument. "Oh, brother," I thought. "Not another door-to-door salesman trying to hawk his musical wares." I was always being approached by someone or other trying to sell me something bizarre. The guy's name was Paul Beaver and he told me of this new musical thing called a

Moog synthesizer. I was entranced. "You mean it can create any sound in the universe?" I asked incredulously. "Any sound at all," Paul replied confidently. I *had* to have one.

A few weeks later, we were in the studio recording a Carole King tune called "Star Collector." Mike was on guitar, Peter on keyboards, and I was on the Moog synthesizer, a huge, multi-tiered console of knobs, buttons, plugs, switches, and patch cords. At the time, all I could do was make it sound like a flying saucer, so that's what I did. (To my knowledge, that was the first time that a synthesizer had been used on a pop record.)

Amidst all of this, the entire Monkees production company flew to France to film an episode of "Monkees in Paris" (where *The Monkees* wasn't even on the air). The PTB must have figured that Paris was probably the only city around where we could film without being hassled to death. They were right. Not only weren't we hassled, the French didn't have any bloody idea who we were at all. All they knew was that there were these idiot Americans running around their fair city and causing monstrous traffic jams at the Arc de Triomphe. (It's funny, but one of my most distinct memories of this trip is of running frantically down the Champs-Elysées with a bad case of diarrhea and not knowing how to say "bathroom" in French.)

The day after filming wrapped up, we were off to London where, that very night, we headlined the first of five sold-out concerts at the Wembley Arena. Simultaneously, my song "Alternate Title" was number two on the English charts.

This time (try though they did), the press had been totally unable to even put a tiny dent in the Magnificent Monkee Machine. We took the country by storm. We stayed at the Royal Kensington Gardens Hotel and, day and night, there were hundreds of screaming, crying, singing kids under our windows, blocking the sidewalks and stopping traffic in the street. Every once in a while, one of us would "throw them a bone" and consent to make an appearance on a balcony. When we did so, the steady drone of, "We love the Monkees" became a thunderous roar that rattled the windows and rattled our brains. Apparently there was someone else being rattled too, because one night, late, Bob Rafelson came into my room to show me a note, a *royal* note. It was from Princess Margaret, who lived just down the "street" in Kensington Palace. It read something like:

Dear Sirs:
Could you please arrange for your arduous admirers to refrain from their boisterous plaudits as it is very difficult for one to get one's sleep.
HRH Princess Margaret.

I was virtually a prisoner in my hotel in those days. It was impossible to go anywhere without an entourage and a dozen assorted minders. I was completely isolated from the outside world. The hotel became a space station. That is why I was not surprised one afternoon to find Brian Jones of the Stones hiding out in one of our rooms. It seems that one of our minders had recently been one of his minders, and when Brian got busted for pot, someone got the bright idea to hide him in the Monkees' hotel! Who would look for him there? They were right. No one looked. (I wonder what the statute of limitations is for harboring a fugitive?) That night, during our concert, we all wore black armbands to protest the jailing of Mick Jagger and Keith Richards for this same string of drug busts.

Even before I had time to recover from the British tour, I was hustled back to Los Angeles to start our American tour. I only had a couple of days to unpack, wash my underwear, repack, feed my dog, and then I was on my way back to the airport. But this time I wasn't flying commercially. In the interests of expense, convenience, and ego, the PTB had decided that it would be in the best interests of all if we just chartered our own plane instead of having to worry about departure times, arrival times, and trying to keep our band of crazies from getting spread out all over this great land of ours.

So, on the day of departure, I pulled up onto the tarmac at

LAX, got out of my limo, and stepped onto the Monkee Express, a four-engine DC9 complete with Monkee logo displayed prominently on the side, a custom-designed interior complete with "lounge" area, kitchen, sleepers, and two mod stewardesses clad in Monkee Express miniskirts.

The plane was loaded up, I got loaded up, and off we went into the wild blue yonder. We kicked off the tour in Atlanta on July 7, 1967. As promised, our opening act was the Jimi Hendrix Experience.

A lot's been said about Jimi Hendrix opening for us and let me make it perfectly clear, as Tricky Dicky said, I am quite sure that Jimi Hendrix would have done very well, with or without appearing on that Monkees tour. Like they say, "You can't keep a good band down." But I was delighted that he had joined us, and thrilled when he eventually broke his first record and rocketed to stardom. And if I, in even the smallest way, contributed to his success, then I am honored.

But being an opening act on any major tour is very difficult at best. Let's face it, the vast majority of the audience is there to see the headliner. And pop fans, especially young ones, can get very impatient. Not long ago I saw Guns N' Roses open for the Stones and get hammered; you can imagine what it must have been like for an act like Jimi Hendrix opening for the Monkees.

But Jimi was not just your ordinary opening act. It was evident from the start that we were witness to a rare and phenomenal talent. Jimi was virtually the only act that I ever made a point of getting to the hall early to see. I would stand in the wings and watch, and listen, in awe. I feel incredibly lucky just to have been there.

Unfortunately, it did became rather awkward, almost comical. Jimi would amble out onto the stage, fire up the amps, and break into "Purple Haze," and the kids in the audience would instantly drown him out with, "We want Daaavy!" God, was it embarrassing.

It wasn't the kids' fault. They simply wanted to see their

idols. The real problems started with the parents who had *brought* the kids. They were probably not too crazy about having to sit through a "godawful" Monkee concert anyway, much less see this black guy in a psychedelic Day-Glo blouse, playing music from hell, holding his guitar like he was fucking it, then lighting it on fire. Presumably, the PTB got some very nasty letters from the Daughters of the American Revolution who were "disgusted" by Mr. Hendrix's performance. Silly cows. I'll bet Alexander Hamilton and Thomas Jefferson would have *loved* Jimi Hendrix.

Jimi didn't stay on the tour for long. "Purple Haze" was breaking and he was getting offers to headline his own concerts. That, along with the fact that ten-year-old girls and their straight-laced parents were not exactly his audience, must have convinced him it was time to make a move. He asked to be released from his contract and the PTB naturally consented. I was very sorry to see him go. But before he left, we did have some great times: running around the New York City psychedelic scene like kids in a candy store, tripping at the Electric Circus and jamming until all hours of the night in the hotel room with Peter and his buddy Stephen Stills.

Jimi was just a kid, like me—a little naive, somewhat innocent, and a musical genius (unlike me). His premature death was such a tragic accident. Like so many of my contemporaries there was just too much available, too fast, too cheap. And with no one around to tell them what was safe and what wasn't, they were like guinea pigs, subject to the experimental whim of any would-be chemist who was trying to make a fortune by designing the latest new, improved chemical shortcut to serenity, amusement, or wisdom. I don't know how it happened, but somewhere along the line I must have had some sort of governor installed that protected me from going too far, too fast. Maybe it was my upbringing. Maybe, like my mom says, it was a guardian angel, or maybe I was just lucky.

By this point, our stage show was getting very frustrating.

We were really starting to cook as a band, but who the hell could hear us? This was long before the advent of sophisticated rock & roll sound systems, and I was lucky if I could hear *myself* play, much less the other guys. The audiences probably heard even less. Of course the reviewers, who were looking for any excuse they could find to trash us, invariably accused us of miming to tapes or using a band backstage or some other bullshit. (If the truth be known, I suspect that our critics were just getting *so* pissed off because no matter *what* they said, it didn't make any bloody difference. We just kept right on a'coming.)

Besides us, the production people, and Hendrix and Co., the Monkee Express plane soon became laden with friends, lovers, friends of lovers, and the various and sundry accessories that make up any respectable rock & roll outfit.

At one time or another, Stephen Stills, David Crosby, Peter Fonda, and a host of others joined us for a jaunt here or a jaunt there on our tour plane. And we had one very special guest on board, thanks to Davy Jones's admirable good will—Jan Berry of Jan & Dean. Davy had met Jan just before the tour and had felt that the traveling, the people, and the activity of the tour would help Jan cope with the incredibly difficult task of recovering from his horrific automobile accident; an accident that virtually ended his successful recording career and shattered his personal dream of getting a medical degree. For my money, it worked. He came on tour unable to speak, hardly able to walk, and by the end of the trip he was carrying on conversations, dancing, and singing along with the band. Hats off to Davy Jones.

As you can imagine, having all these "heavy" people on board the Monkee Express guaranteed that there was never a dull moment. The seats in the back of the plane had been taken out and replaced with lounges and pillows, so this naturally became the local hangout—our version of "10-Forward." This was where all the party animals would gather and do the things that only party animals can do so well. Those who didn't want to know, or had partied themselves into a stupor, sat up front in "coach."

This back section used to get a lot of business, and one night, somewhere over the great American prairie, a message came back from the Captain. He was requesting that some of the passengers in the back of the plane move to the front of the plane because he was trying to land and couldn't get the nose of the plane down.

What a tour. Samantha joined me for part of it, and we continued to fall deeper and deeper in love. We didn't talk about it much, but it was evident that things had gone way past the stage of a casual affair. I just couldn't imagine not being with her. We were as thick as thieves.

At the end of August, the tour ended. Abruptly. One day I was high-flying it, fast-balling it, rockin' and rollin' around the countryside on the Monkee Express, and the next I found myself back in old Los Angeles, back in the old makeup chair on the old soundstage, getting my hair curled by the same old Hollywood hairdresser with the same old cigarette hanging out of her mouth. It was straight out of the *Twilight Zone*. From the roar of the crowds and the smell of the aviation fuel to the roar of the assistant director and the smell of the electricians. What a shock.

And if you thought we were hard to handle before, you should have seen us now. We were like wild animals that had been roaming free on the African savannah and suddenly found themselves transported to a pet shop in Duluth.

The second season of *The Monkees* brought several changes. Gone was the JCPenney wardrobe, gone were the conventional Monkee suits and shirts. Now it was Nehru jackets, love beads, and, in my case, a wild head of Afro hair. Before the tour we'd been isolated, cosseted, protected from the elements. But now we'd partaken of the forbidden fruit. We'd seen it all and done it all: Paris, London, New York, high-society, low-society, hanging with the intelligentsia, freaking with the famous and the infamous. Our corporeal selves had landed at LAX, but the essence of our celestial beings had made a quantum jump into a higher orbit. Never, really, to come down again.

It was no longer possible to contain us in our custom-made dressing rooms—they were too close to the set and you couldn't tell a Monkee to be quiet! (There was also this problem of the occasional smell of burning weeds wafting across the studio lot.) So someone had the brilliant idea of building us a special holding pen (or reactor core containment device, if you prefer). Out in back of the stage, well away from the prying eyes, ears, and noses of the curious, they constructed this big, soundproof, windowless, air-conditioned black box. It had only one door with a huge meat locker handle. This is where we would return between takes to rejuvenate, like vampires. Here, we would relax, party, or just be cool. The only things in the room were a few pillows and a few candles, but on one wall was a bank of four 150-watt lightbulbs with each of our names underneath. Whenever the assistant director (a wonderful man named John Anderson) needed one of us he would flip a switch on the stage and, inside the box, the appropriate bulb would light up. Of course, after spending a couple of hours in this dark, cool cavern, a 150-watt lightbulb has relatively the same effect on your eyeballs as a supernova. I recall, more than once, being blasted out of my reverie by this device and stumbling onto the set blinded and dazed. In a funny way, that seemed to work to our advantage. Bob and Bert had invested a lot of time and energy to create this spontaneous environment for us to thrive in, and this "fish-out-of-water" flavor only added to the effect. If you watch the show carefully, it often appears that we have just landed in the scene from outer space—which isn't too far from the truth.

There were only a few select people who could really get close to me in these days. I did not suffer fools easily. One I admired was John Anderson, the assistant director I mentioned. He was about the only man on the planet that I respected enough to heed; and there was Henry Diltz, the famous rock photographer (many of the photos in this book are courtesy of Henry). Henry and I spent many happy hours wandering around the catwalks above the soundstages at Columbia Pictures, like phantoms of the filmstage, spying on the other productions and musing about life, love, lust, and the latest lot of lovely ladies.

As far as the series went, we were also trying to get a little more ambitious. The NBC censorship office had always vetoed anything even the slightest bit controversial, and I know that Bob and Bert continually fought with them about one issue or the other. On the whole, the internal censorship didn't bother me much because I didn't feel that *The Monkees* was really the platform to mount political or social views. But I think that all of us, at one time or the other, would have liked to have made a statement about certain topics: the war, for instance. We simply were not allowed to do so unless it was in the lightest or most innocuous way. (Funnily enough, our first hit song, "Last Train to Clarksville," was an antiwar song about a soldier going off to war.)

But one particular episode brought the whole issue of censorship to a head. The episode was "The Devil and Peter Tork." It was based, loosely, on *The Devil and Daniel Webster* and, having to do with the Devil, of course there was the occasional mention of the word "hell." The network refused to even let us mention the word! Bob and Bert really went to bat on this one, and we managed to make a joke of it on the show. That should give you some idea of the national sociopolitical atmosphere that prevailed at the time. (This is what frightens me about the mores of the current "politically correct" movement and its penchant for censorship. Censorship by any other name is still censorship.)

We were really pushing the envelope during the second season. We started trying different styles of production and invited unusual guest stars like Frank Zappa and Tim Buckley to perform. And we really started to stretch out on the music video front. I've been asked many times if I think the Monkees were the founders of the music video. My standard answer is, "I think it's dangerous to claim paternity in these cases." Cutting film to music has been around for a long time (they use to call them "musicals"). The Beatles sang and ran around in *A Hard Day's Night* and *Help;* the Marx Brothers did it in virtually every movie they ever made; Laurel and Hardy did it; Presley did it; Ricky Nelson use to sing a song at the end of *Ozzie and Harriet.* But there's no question that *The Monkees* took the form to new heights and, in particular, used the "romps," as we used to call them, to promote our songs on television and tie them into radio play and record sales. (Ironically, I can't *stand* watching music videos anymore.)

The highlight of the second season for me was to take the helm and direct one of the episodes, "The Frodis Caper." John Anderson and I had come up with the idea and we got Dave Evans, one of the Monkee staff writers, to pen the script. I hadn't had any formal training as a director, but just being around a set all my life had taught me a lot. I must have just picked up a lot of what I needed to know through osmosis because I breezed through the shooting schedule and finished a half a day early. Little did I know at the time that this directing exercise would set me up for a very successful future in film and television production. I must thank Bob and Bert for giving me that shot.

Quite frankly, we were getting a little jaded with the show as it existed. Every week Davy would fall in love with some girl, or Peter would be kidnapped by some bad guy, or some spy would hide his microfilm in somebody's something or other. The very intense, improvisational quality that had ignited the show in the first place was burning so fast it was threatening to consume the very beings who had created it.

We started talking about what we would do on the next season—a live show? a variety show? just a series of sketches? (One idea that came up was an awful lot like *Laugh-In,* a show that aired a year or so later.) The network, of course, was saying,

"If it ain't broke don't fix it." Our ratings were still good and the conventional wisdom was that you shouldn't change Monkees in midseason. But we were adamant: "The only thing that doesn't change is change itself," said one of us philosophically (probably Peter). Unfortunately, we never had to worry about pushing the issue. At the end of the second season, and by mutual consent, *The Monkees* was cancelled.

You might think that we would have been devastated. Especially me, who knew the power that the tube could wield. But I had been as deluded by the grandeur as had everyone else. "So, our series is cancelled. Who cares? Do we? No way. We are huge. The Beatles are bigger than Christ? Well we're even bigger than the Beatles! Just look at *Billboard* magazine!"

We didn't need the networks, we didn't need television, we didn't need the record companies, or the radio stations, the fan magazines, food, water, or oxygen. We could go on forever just feeding off of ourselves. The Monster Monkee Music and Madness Machine was indestructible!

What we needed was a lobotomy.

In the midst of all this, we had been talking about making a movie. It had seemed like the logical thing to do since we were so fucking enormous. But what to do? What kind of movie could possible capture the immenseness, the prodigiousness, the wonderfulness, the glory that was us?

One day, Bob and Bert introduced us to a guy Bob had become friendly with and who was going to help write our movie. He was a B-movie actor at the time, but he had much greater aspirations, one of them screenwriting. His name was Jack Nicholson.

Nine

No More Monkee Business

....

Whoever battles with monsters had better see that it does not turn him into a monster. And if you gaze long into an abyss, the abyss will gaze back into you.

—Friedrich Nietzsche

When Bob, Bert, and the four of us started discussing the making of the Monkees movie, it was generally agreed that we didn't just want to make a ninety-minute version of one of our TV shows. That would be predictable and, besides, we were getting pretty fed up with the standard Monkee sitcom format. Columbia Pictures was putting up the money (a grand total of $750,000), and I don't know what they were expecting, but since Bert's father was the president of the company, who cared?

In retrospect, we probably *should* have just made a ninety-minute version of the TV show; it would have been much more commercial, but "hindsight is always . . . ," etc. Anyway, I'm very proud of the film we eventually did make—*Head*.

So, Bob introduces us to Jack Nicholson, and we all fall in

love with him immediately. He's young, hip, cool, charismatic, funny, wise, intelligent; all of those things that he still is today (except young).

We all agreed that he would be the perfect partner for our film project, and one weekend in the midst of filming the TV series and recording new tracks, the seven of us set off for a golf resort in Ojai, California. It was there that we were going to pool all of our ideas, inspirations, dreams, visions, wants and needs, and flesh out the movie concept. We all got little rooms adjoining the golf course (none of us actually played golf) and started the long round of "discussions" that would eventually become the film.

We sat around for days smoking (but we didn't inhale), drinking (but we didn't swallow), and generally having stream of consciousness sessions about television, movies, music, art, love, lust, good, bad, evil, life, and death. You know, small talk. To be honest, I don't remember a word of what was said, but it must have been pretty weird because Jack and Bob took the tapes of the sessions and turned them into one of the strangest films of all time.

The weekend trip did not go without incident, however. When the time came to discuss writing credit, we were informed that only Jack and Bob would be given credit. We were disappointed and angry. Mike was furious. He took all the tapes and locked them in the trunk of his car! After a few days of "negotiations" the tapes were returned, but we didn't get any credit. Oh well, onward and upward.

Jack did a great job on the screenplay. To this day, I'm not sure what it's all about; I'm not even sure if *he* is. But it was certainly provocative.

Basically, it was the story of the Monkees: our birth, life, and death, as metaphors for all of Hollywood and its tinsel-and-fabric manipulations of people, images, and ideas. And it was loaded with inside jokes from the perspective of a Hollywooder.

There's no doubt that Bob Rafelson's and Jack Nicholson's personal perceptions heavily colored the finished product.

As was becoming the norm, even the making of the movie was to have its problems, at least initially. Right from the beginning of the television series, there had been a dispute over our salaries. Time and time again, Bob and Bert would put their arms around our shoulders and . . . you remember.

Since we didn't have any powerful representatives, either individually or collectively, we never got very far; just the promise of a "bigger slice of the cake" when it was eventually out of the oven. But our weekly salaries continued to stay low, we participated in only a fraction of the tour revenues, and the merchandising was nonexistent. "When the hell is this cake going to be done?" we cried in anguish. The only area in which we were making any money was record royalties, and I suspect that the PTB would have liked a little bit more of that if they could have had it. So, when the movie came along, we decided to renegotiate.

It was Mike, naturally, who took the lead and introduced us to Jerry Perenchio—a very powerful agent in Hollywood at the time. Jerry took us on and promised he would cut us a very lucrative deal. The only problem was that we would have to stick to our guns, make a stand, even *strike* if it became necessary. It did. I don't remember what we were asking for, it couldn't have been much; yet Bob and Bert wouldn't give in. We didn't have many choices open to us: either hold firm or cave in. And to make matters worse, Peter had decided that he was not going to join us. Peter! The antiestablishment, anticapitalistic antianti. Here we were, the *workers,* lined up at the barricades, ready to take on the opulent potentates, and Peter sided with the parsimonious PTB! He was a scab! Good heavens!

The first day of shooting came along and there was only one Monkee on the set: Peter. "Here I come . . . walking down the street . . ."

But by the next day we were all back. The deal had been done, the negotiations finalized. Unfortunately, even after all the millions that Bob and Bert had made off of the Monkees, I don't think they ever forgave us for standing up to them that one time. Oh well, onward and . . .

Filming that movie was one of the high points of my career. Bob Rafelson was directing it, Jack Nicholson had written it, how could you go wrong? The supporting cast was certainly the most eclectic that had ever been assembled: Annette Funicello, Victor Mature, Sonny Liston, Teri Garr, Carol Doda, Peter Fonda, Dennis Hopper, and Frank Zappa. Frank Zappa's involvement was interesting since he had already appeared on our television show and was probably one of the only hip people around who knew what the hell we were doing. (Frank would eventually ask me if I wanted to be the drummer for the Mothers of Invention. I called the PTB but, unfortunately, I was still under contract with RCA Records and they wouldn't let me go. I often wonder what would have happened if . . . ?)

The film was choreographed by Toni Basil, and featured wonderful songs by Carole King, Harry Nilsson, Peter, and Mike. One of my favorite Carole King songs of all time, "As We Go Along," is in that movie, featuring the guitar work of Ry Cooder and Neil Young.

There was action, thrills, adventure, sex, horror, slapstick, beautiful scenery, and state-of-the-art visual effects, including, to my knowledge, the first use of "solarization" (that saturated negative colorizing hippie trippie photographic technique). This film was a hippie's wet dream. Kind of like *Hellzapoppin* meets Peter Max.

We filmed all over the western United States, and then Jack and I made a special trip to the Bahamas to film the underwater mermaid sequences. Jack and I got along great. If there ever was a man who appreciated the finer things in life more than I, especially the fine feminine form, it was Sir Jack.

Now, the Bahamas were *very* formal back then, and the

dress code for the casinos was strictly coat and tie. Jack and I, naturally, didn't own a coat and tie between us.

Cut to:

Ext. Paradise Island Casino—Night

Jack and Micky are swaggering up the moonlit path to the old colonial building. They are dressed to kill in their brocade Nehru jackets, paisley bell-bottom trousers, and multicolored love beads. The sweet scent of tropical flowers fills the air; somewhere a cricket rubs its legs together in a soulful mating cry.

They bound up the marble steps, swing open the heavy oak door, and enter into the bustling, opulent casino. The sights and sounds of the jet set at play taunt and beckon them. They look around with an air of cool disinterest. Suddenly, a VERY LARGE MAN in a tuxedo appears out of nowhere. He looks the two young studs over with some disdain. Micky and Jack think he's a waiter.

JACK

Hey, good buddy. Howya doing? I'll have a double Jack Daniel's and . . .

LARGE MAN

I'm afraid that a coat and *tie* are required to enter the casino, *sir.*

Jack and Micky look down at their very expensive East Indian jackets.

MICKY

These *are* coats. They're . . .

LARGE MAN
(interrupting)

Only *formal* attire is permitted inside this establishment, *sir.*

Micky, being the nonconfrontational sort, starts to turn away. Jack, being the confrontational sort, bravely stands his ground.

JACK

Wait a minute. You're telling me that only *formal* clothes are allowed in here?

LARGE MAN
(impatiently)

Yes, sir. Now if you'll . . .

He starts to usher Jack out. Big Mistake.

JACK

Wait a fucking minute! These jackets *are* formal attire you cretin. These jackets are *Nehru* jackets. Named after the Prime Minister of fucking *India.* These jackets were formal attire all over the fucking world. These jackets were formal attire when your ancestors were picking berries and shitting in the woods!

Fade Out

. . . we had a great time in the casino that night.

When *Head* was released in November of 1968, it was met with mixed reviews. Most of the serious movie critics didn't even bother to see it because they thought it was going to be just like the TV show. A few critics loved it. The fans, however, hated it. Or, rather, they just didn't understand it. Regrettably, we had left them in the dust. Because the film was rated R, most of our fans couldn't even get into the theater to see it in the first place, and those who did just didn't have any idea of what we were up to.

There was this one very disturbing sequence in which Bob used that famous piece of news footage of Vietnamese General Nguyen Ngoc Loan pulling out a snub-nosed .38 and shooting Vietcong Captain Bay Lop in the head. It has been argued that that image profoundly altered American public opinion about what was actually at stake in the war, and Bob used it to death (no pun intended). At one point in the movie it is shown thirty-two times simultaneously in split screen.

One day after the film had been released, I was standing around at a car wash waiting for my little red Mercedes 280 SL to get out of the bath when this fifteen- or sixteen-year-old girl comes up and starts berating me about how I was "glorifying the war and condoning the killing!" She thought that by showing that footage in the movie we were somehow *endorsing* the war instead of decrying it. Needless to say, I was dumbfounded. But it did make me realize how far we had come, or rather how far we had gone from our original intentions and design.

On the home front, I had made a big decision. I'd asked Samantha to come and live with me in Los Angeles. She graciously consented. We hadn't talked about marriage much, but we did know that we wanted to be together. The word "marriage" was kind of verboten in those days and in those circles. It was too . . . conventional. The prevailing attitude was something like, "Two spirits that are meant to be one shouldn't have to condescend to such an archaic orthodox tradition." (God, did I *really* think like that?) We had even gone so far as to avoid using the word "love," it was just too . . . establishment. We coined a new word to describe how we felt about each other: "gleeb." We would be standing there, holding hands, she in her custom-coordinated miniskirt outfit and I in my cutoff jeans and tie-dyed T-shirt, and look into each other's eyes and say, "I gleeb you!"

So she packed up her bags and her Siamese cat, checked out of her London flat, and headed west, knowing not what to expect.

I met her at the airport in a limo, naturally, and she must have thought, "Wow, this is certainly going to be something!" Little did she know that I really hated limos and thought of them as just glorified taxicabs. The limo took us straight to the studio where I transferred her luggage into my beat-up VW minibus and took her up to my new house nestled deep in the Hollywood Hills.

What a shock it must have been for this girl. One day she is popping around London, in and out of Harrods, whizzing 'round Piccadilly Circus, lunch at the Dorchester, tea at the Ritz, and the next day she moves into a four-story, Hollywood Hills hippie halfway house, decorated by garage sale, furnished by Sears Craftsman, and peopled by my assorted friends, fellow tripping travelers, hangers-on, and the two stewardesses from the Monkee Express! Talk about your culture shock. A couple of nights after she arrived, she gathered up the courage to venture downstairs into the dimly lit basement to do some laundry. She found a pile of dirty clothes on the floor and was about to pick them up when she realized it wasn't a pile of dirty clothes at all, it was a friend of mine sleeping on the floor by the warmth of the gas-fired dryer!

But, to her credit, she kept a stiff British upper lip and adapted well to her posting among the heathen tribes. She soon had the house in shipshape and Bristol fashion and we started having parties. I mean real *parties!*

A sixties' party in Laurel Canyon *usually* meant Red Mountain wine, pretzels, potato chips, and onion dip. But Samantha wouldn't have any of that. Like any good colonial viceroy, she had brought a little bit of England with her, and was eager to share it with everyone. When we had a party, *everyone* came: Jack Nicholson, John Lennon, Marc Bolan, Keith Moon, Harry Nilsson, Beau Bridges, Jeff Bridges, Jim Morrison, Ringo Starr, Donovan, Mama Cass, Brian Wilson, George Harrison, Buddy Miles, Alice Cooper, Carole King, Peter Fonda, Sal Mineo, Harry Dean Stanton, Stephen Stills, David Cassidy, Graham Nash, Joni Mitchell, Linda Ronstadt, Stevie Winwood, Albert Brooks, Don Johnson, and God only knows who else I can't even remember. Don't kid yourselves, these people didn't come to see *me,* they came for a breath of the genteel, cultured sophistication that Samantha brought to the West Coast and to our affluent but rather primordial existence.

It wasn't long before Samantha "had one in the oven." We hadn't talked about having children, just like we hadn't talked about marriage. It was just understood that we would eventually have a family, and since we weren't doing anything to interfere with the biology of it, the eventuality became a reality.

I was ecstatic. A baby! My progeny! Heir to the throne! Child of my loins! Me . . . a father? What would I wear?

We eventually bowed to the wishes of our respective families (thankfully) and decided to get married after all: Hippie convention be damned. And what a beautiful wedding it was. High up in the Hollywood Hills at my Swiss chalet, my stepfather conducting the service, just close friends and family in attendance, Rick Klein, my best man, Coco as maid of honor, and everyone standing around on a carpet of gardenia petals. The stuff of dreams.

Meanwhile, back on the job, we had released another album, *The Birds, the Bees & the Monkees,* and four more singles, "Pleasant Valley Sunday," "Words," "Daydream Believer," and "Valleri." They all did well, sold lots of copies, and I hung more Gold records on my walls. However, the record sales weren't anything like they had been in the past.

Since *The Monkees* TV show had ceased production but was still a top-rated show in reruns, NBC-TV offered us a series of TV specials. The first hour-long special—in a projected series of three—was taped in the summer of 1968. Entitled *33⅓ Revolutions Per Monkee,* the end result was such a disaster that it was the only one ever produced.

For the most part, it was a case of good intentions gone bad. We had all gone off in our own separate directions musically, writing, producing, and singing on our own tracks, so the special was put together without much input from the four of us. The PTB hired a well-known TV producer named Jack Good to helm the project and, for what it's worth, he made it very much his own.

There was quite an impressive lineup of guest stars: Little Richard, Fats Domino, Jerry Lee Lewis, the Buddy Miles Express, the Clara Ward Singers, Brian Auger, and Julie Driscoll, and along with all the stars was a lot of style. Unfortunately, there was little substance. Bob and Bert must have still been hung up on this manufactured Monkee business because, like the movie *Head,* that motif became the theme of the special. But instead of coming across as satirical and whimsical, it reeked of cynicism and spite.

All of this was compounded by formidable production problems. Jack Good was experimenting with the new technique called "chroma key," which enabled one image to be seamlessly combined with another (now the stuff of everyday news programs, but *big* news at the time), and just days before the taping, the musicians at NBC went on strike so we couldn't tape at the studios proper. He had to load up all the video and sound equipment in moving vans and set up production at MGM Studios on an old soundstage. (If I'm not mistaken, that was one of the first, albeit undesired, mobile video productions ever attempted.)

To say that the special did not live up to everyone's expectations would be a gross understatement. NBC liked it so much they put it on against the Academy Awards!

If you had been standing on the outside looking in, you wouldn't have had to have been a rocket scientist to notice that all was not well in Monkeeland. From the commercial failure of *Head* to the failure failure of *33⅓ Revolutions Per Monkee* to the progressive decline in record sales, it must have been obvious to many that the beast that Bob and Bert had created was dying a slow death and needed to be put out of its misery. It was Peter who would mercifully deal the creature a final death blow.

Cut to:

Ext. Mike Nesmith's Hilltop House—Day

The house is barely visible behind a tall security fence. "FRAK," a huge attack-trained German Shepherd is patroling the inside perimeter. You can occasionally see his cold, savage eyes peering out through the cyclone fencing.

Cut To:

Int. House—Day

Micky, Peter, and Davy are sitting around the wet bar that borders the indoor/outdoor pool. Micky is staring out the window, daydreaming, Davy is doing his nails, Peter is shifting about nervously.

MIKE
(slow drawl)

Hey, did you guys see that new four-wheel-drive pick-up truck in *Car and Driver*?

DAVY

Does anybody have an emery board?

MICKY
(wistfully)

Wouldn't it be neat if, like, a flying saucer came down and, like, landed in your yard and . . .

PETER
(gravely)

Guys . . . I'm quitting the group.

All eyes turn to Peter. Is he joking? His eyes say not. Micky, Mike, and Davy exchange glances. Nobody knows what to say. Finally, Mike breaks the silence.

MIKE

Well, good buddy. You gotta do what you gotta do.

Fade Out

Now, you might have thought there would have been some display of histrionics, some attempt at objection, at least a little surprise: "Peter! You can't mean it!" "Please don't leave!" "What will we do without you?"

Nope, 'fraid not. I wasn't surprised at all. Peter had never gotten over his disappointment when we decided not to go back into the studio and work together as we had on *Headquarters*. He even cited that as his main reason for resigning. But I suspect there were other influences as well. The truth was, we were all living in the eye of a hurricane. The world was falling apart around us, the winds of change were tossing our careers and our lives around like so many paper puppets, and, for the most part, we were oblivious to it all.

If the truth be known, the day Peter quit was probably the happiest day of Mike's life. They'd never really gotten along, right from day one. Mike had always perceived of Peter as untenable, and they'd always been adversarial, if not outright combative. *Finally* he was out of the way. Now Mike could get on with doing what he had always wanted to do, make the Monkees *his* group.

And I was happy to go along. I respected Mike and his music and was quite prepared to go along for the ride. I was flourishing as a writer/producer myself, and I saw Peter's abdication as a minor setback at most. Basically, I think the three of us really thought that we would be able to go on, just as we had before, and nobody would even notice there were only three people on stage instead of four—after all Peter didn't sing on many of the songs anyway. How naive.

There comes a time in the history of virtually every group when one or more of its members decide to cut the cord, jump out of the nest, and attempt to fly on their own: Sting, David Lee Roth, David Gates, George Michael, Mick Jagger, Keith Richards, Michael Jackson, Kenny Rogers, etc. Sometimes they make it on their own, sometimes not. In our case, we *all* thought that we could, at any time, just step away from the Monkees and be just as successful, just as powerful, just as desirable. How naive.

I suppose it depends on whom you talk to, but as far as I'm

concerned, the day Peter quit was the day the music died (apologies to Don McLean). Ironically, we had finally coerced the creative control from the PTB, we were making albums that were satisfying and personal (though, admittedly, not selling nearly as well), we were affluent and happily married (I speak for myself), and quite suddenly it was over. Finis. Terminated. It's a wrap. It was the classic case of snatching defeat from the jaws of victory.

I'm making these observations, of course, with the advantage of years of hindsight. At the time, none of this even crossed my mind. The knock-on effect that all of this would have on my professional and personal life would not be felt for some time to come. Life went on as usual for me. In fact, it was going on *better* than usual. Now that I wasn't working on the TV show sixteen hours a day or recording in the studio all weekend, I had time to enjoy some of the fruits of my labors. And enjoy them I did:

- My new bride and I started throwing rounds and rounds of parties.

- We traveled around the States and around the world.

- I started playing celebrity tennis with Bill Cosby, Clint Eastwood, Merv Griffin, Robert Duvall, Andy Williams, and Dabney Coleman (who is an awesome tennis player).

- I learned to play golf with this rock singer who lived next door named Vince Furnier (who later changed his name to Alice Cooper).

- Alice and I eventually started a softball team called the Hollywood Vampires.

- I climbed Mount Whitney.

- I built a gyrocopter in my den and went out to the Mohave Desert to fly it (then I realized how dangerous it was so I sold it).

- I obtained one of the first domestic-use lasers on the West Coast and used it as a lighting effect for my parties.

- I started experimenting with holography.

- I bought two *very* expensive antique cars in England and tooled around Hollywood like the Great Gatsby, until one of them rolled down my driveway and was totaled.

- I hung out at Peter's where he was running a macrobiotic halfway house for wayward hippies and naked nubile nymphs (where we sat around the pool and listened as Stephen Stills played his guitar and sang this "new" song he had written called "For What It's Worth").

- I hung out at Davy's where this friend of his named Charlie Smalls played us songs from the new musical he was trying to get produced called *The Wiz.*

- I built a recording studio in my garage with the help and guidance of Samantha's wonderful father, Les, and started having basement sessions with the likes of John Lennon, Marc Bolan, Harry Nilsson, Buddy Miles, Brian Wilson, and Alice Cooper.

- I chased flying saucer reports around the California desert with my very good friend Elliot Mintz (who would go on to become public relations representative for the likes of John and Yoko and Don Johnson.)

- I started writing and developing TV and movie ideas with the very talented writer Bill Martin (who lived next door to Harry Dean Stanton and underneath Linda Ronstadt).

- I wandered around L.A. with my 16mm camera documenting the life and times of southern California circa 1969 (including a far-out birthday party for Mama Cass featuring a very young Eric Clapton).

- I had weekly table tennis tournaments that Beau Bridges would *always* win.

- I smoked a couple of square miles of Colombia (the country not the studio).

- I spent money like it was going out of style and drove my poor mom crazy by never keeping receipts.

- I rode around like an idiot on my 650 Triumph Bonneville, screaming down the Ventura Freeway at 90 mph wearing just a bathing suit and dark glasses!

- I generally just rested on my laurels in Laurel Canyon and wallowed in the affluence that the Monkees experience had afforded me.

- And right in the middle of all this insanity along came one of the happiest days of my life: the birth of Ami Bluebell Dolenz. I filmed it, naturally.

Ami was born on January 8, 1969, and quickly became the center of our attention and the light of my life. Samantha had, very wisely, imported her parents to live with us, and they provided a very solid home base for Ami (and for us also I might add). I was pretty crazy back then and, what with all the traveling around and the general insanity of the times, much of Ami's strength of character and good sense can be attributed to the stability that Samantha's mum and dad (Phylis and Les) brought to our household.

A good friend of mine at the time was a young English lad named Brenden Cahil. Talk about your success stories: Brenden had been my limo driver during my first trip to London. He had been very helpful to me, so at the end of the trip I thought I would surprise him and buy him a motorcycle. He graciously declined the offer explaining that, what with the English weather, he would probably just end up killing himself. Instead, he asked if he could get a one-way ticket to visit the States. I

"White man come to Indian land, killum wife, rapeum buffalo." (FESTIVAL NEWS SERVICE/MARK BEGO COLLECTION)

From paltry JCPenney promotions to repulsive, paisley apparel. (HENRY DILTZ)

Documenting the 1967 Mexican
Grand Prix. An auteur is born.
(HENRY DILTZ)

At the height of
Monkeemania in 1967.
(HENRY DILTZ)

During the second season of the show, we started becoming restless with the
constraints of network television. (HENRY DILTZ)

With Teri Garr in the Monkees movie, *Head*. (RAYBERT PRODUCTIONS/MJB ARCHIVES)

On the set of *Head* with Victor Mature. Davy is working hard on copping Victor's smile. (RAYBERT PRODUCTIONS/ JOE RUSSO COLLECTION)

With *Head* we were finally able to express our disdain for the war in Vietnam by parodying it. (RAYBERT PRODUCTIONS/MJB ARCHIVES)

Backstage in Salt Lake City, with Jack Nicholson. We were getting ready to film the "Circle Sky" sequence. (HENRY DILTZ)

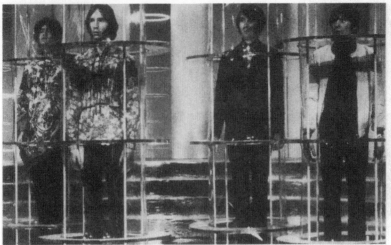

In our 1969 television special, *33⅓ Revolutions Per Monkee*. This was our final project as a quartet. I'm still wearing the tablecloth. (SCREEN GEMS PRODUCTIONS/STEVE COX COLLECTION)

With Mike and Davy on *The Johnny Cash Show*. We were officially a trio at this point. (ABC-TV/JOE RUSSO COLLECTION)

Samantha gave up her career in British television to move to L.A. to be with me. (MICKY DOLENZ)

Samantha and I totally in "gleeb," with little Ami. (JOE RUSSO COLLECTION)

With Harry Nilsson in 1972, at the height of our party animal phase. (MICKY DOLENZ)

When *The Monkees* came to an end in 1970, I worked hard at becoming a token tennis celebrity. The open mouth is so that, if I miss the ball with my racquet, I can catch it between my teeth. (HENRY DILTZ)

With Ami at her tap dancing lessons. (HENRY DILTZ)

In 1976 as Dolenz, Jones, Boyce & Hart. Tommy Boyce and Bobby Hart had written several of the Monkees' biggest hits in the sixties. (CAPITOL RECORDS/MARK BEGO COLLECTION)

Backstage at one of the Monkees' reunion shows in the eighties with Ami. She is now a successful actress in her own right. (HENRY DILTZ)

Bob Rafelson, me, Bert Schneider, Peter, Mike, and Davy, backstage at Universal Amphitheatre in Los Angeles, September 1986. (HENRY DILTZ)

A rare harmonious moment with the four of us in the eighties. (HENRY DILTZ)

With Davy and Peter, during the album cover session for our 1987 LP, *Pool It.* (RHINO RECORDS/MARK BEGO COLLECTION)

Davy, Peter, and I tried our hand at "glam rock" à la Kiss, in one of our *Pool It* videos. (HENRY DILTZ)

The last time the four of us reunited was to be awarded our star on Hollywood Boulevard, July 10, 1989. (HENRY DILTZ)

After twelve years as a successful television director in London, I moved back to Los Angeles to resume my acting and singing career. (HENRY DILTZ)

My daughters, Charlotte, Emily, and Georgia. (AMI DOLENZ COLLECTION)

In 1991 I released my first solo album, *Micky Dolenz Puts You to Sleep*, a collection of children's lullabies. (RHINO RECORDS/MARK BEGO COLLECTION)

agreed, and he joined our entourage. By the time we landed in
the States he had a job as a gofer for the production company
(and was sleeping in my attic); in a year he was a junior executive at Screen Gems Music, and a couple of years later he was
vice president of music at Universal Pictures!

"There's no business like show business . . ."

One of my very best friends at this time was a young
singer/songwriter who had been introduced to me during the
recording of *Headquarters*. He had been working in a bank when
the Monkees decided to record one of his tunes. At that point he
decided to quit the job at the bank and pursue his music career
full-time. The tune we recorded was "Cuddly Toy," and the
singer/songwriter was Harry Nilsson.

Harry and I became very good friends and remain so to this
day. He would come over to my house and play around in the
studio, or we would go over to the neighborhood park to play
basketball, or we'd hike up to the Hollywood sign and scratch
our initials into the celebrated structure, or we would just cruise
around Hollywood on a warm summer "what's it all about
Alfie?" kind of day, waxing philosophical.

Harry had met a beautiful Irish girl named Oona in New
York, and he asked Samantha and me to accompany him to
Ireland to meet her parents. He was going to ask them for her
hand in marriage and apparently thought Samantha and I would
lend some sort of credibility (Samantha maybe . . . but me?).
Poor Harry was so nervous he passed out on the way to their
house, and we had to stop at a hotel to revive him.

Harry was, and still is, one of most intriguing, astute, in-
spired, remarkable men I have ever known. But he can also be
quite a handful. He lives life to the fullest, and if ever there was
a man who lived his life by the dictum "seize the day," it is Harry
Nilsson.

It was quite common for Harry to call me up in the middle
of the day to go out and have "a nice quiet little lunch." Two
days later I would wake up in a massage parlor in San Diego. But

there was one adventure that really took the cake.

One night we were out at a restaurant with our respective wives (Harry's first wife, Diane), and Harry started a conversation with a group of people sitting at another table. When we finished, he invited the newfound friends back over to my house for a drink and to continue their conversation.

Cut to:

Ext. Micky's House—Night (Early Morning)

Micky, Samantha, Harry, and Diane are just getting out of Micky's car in the driveway of Micky's hillside home when they hear a CRASH. They go back down the driveway and discover that two of the people Harry had invited back to the house (two girls) have accidentally sideswiped a neighbor's car on the dark, narrow street.

Within moments, the neighbor, a suspected DRUG DEALER, comes running out of his house.

DRUG DEALER

#@%# . . . my car. &%$ #& . . . you . . . &#@$*&!

HARRY

&%$#$% . . . your car. You &#%$@!

DRUG DEALER

Oh yeah?!

And with that, the crazed long-haired weirdo pulls out a KITCHEN KNIFE! Suddenly, a minor fender bender has become some serious shit. Samantha and Diane quickly disappear into the house as the knife-wielding doper starts to back Harry up Micky's driveway.

HARRY

You . . . &#$@. What are you gonna do, cut me?

DRUG DEALER

I might.

As the crazed maniac is dancing around with Harry, Micky does what any fine red-blooded American man would do in a situation like this . . . escalate! He turns and runs up the driveway to the side door of the house that opens onto Samantha's parents' bedroom.

Cut To:

Ext. Parents' Bedroom—Night

Micky runs up to the door and pounds on it frantically.

MICKY

Les! The gun! I need the gun!

Les stumbles out of bed and opens the door.

LES
(*frightened*)

What? Why? What's bloody happening?

MICKY

Just give me the gun!

Les reaches under the bed and gets the little .22 caliber pistol that Micky had given him to have as protection when he and Samantha are away. Micky grabs the weapon and races back to the front lines.

Cut To:

Ext. Front Lines—Night

The battle rages on; the Drug Dealer is circling Harry, stalking him . . .

HARRY

You . . . &%$#@!

DRUG DEALER

You . . . #%$ $@#!

Suddenly, Micky comes marching down the driveway, the .22 pistol tucked in his pants. The Drug Dealer sees it immediately and stops in his tracks.

DRUG DEALER
(false bravado)

Humph . . . Whaddaya gonna do, shoot me?

MICKY
(his best Clint Eastwood)

I might.

The Drug Dealer backs down, lowers the knife, and retreats back into his house. The bluff has worked. (Or was it a bluff?) No one will ever know. (I've often wondered what would have happened if the Drug Dealer had decided to escalate the confrontation himself and pulled out an Uzi.)

Fade Out

To top it all off, the two girls leave my house to go to the Drug Dealer's house and party! Harry got so mad that he picked up a huge rock and put it through the rear window of their car!

I don't know how Samantha put up with all of this. The late nights, the crazy friends. One time at four in the morning the doorbell goes off, rousing everyone, including infant Ami, out of a deep sleep. It's Buddy Miles and Steve Winwood who want to use the studio to jam. I politely had to turn them away.

Another morning, who shows up but Harry Nilsson and Ringo Starr after a rip-roaring all-nighter. They look absolutely awful (they must have been having a *great* time). They're both stumbling around the house when Samantha offers to make Ringo "chip butty and eggs"—a strange Liverpudlian concoction. He very nearly cries in gratitude. To this day I'm not sure what the hell "chip butty and eggs" are, but it sure set him right.

From that day on he called her "Earth Mother."

Reflecting on our marriage from the vantage point of three decades later—we were really up against terrible odds. It's a credit to Samantha that she managed to hang in there for as long as she did.

And the fans . . . Most of the time my fans were well behaved, discreet, and polite. But, unfortunately, I did have my disturbed admirers just like everyone else. There were these two very nasty girls in particular (you know who you are). They started by following me around in their car, running red lights to keep up with me, and stalking me right up to my house. They soon became braver and started coming up to the front door, ringing the bell, and inventing some lame excuse to get me to come out. I eventually became more and more irritated as they became more wicked and psychotic.

One day they would bring me presents, the next they would steal my mail. One day they would pledge eternal devotion, the next day they would poison my pets. The closest I come to describing their joint personalities is the Annie Wilkes character in *Misery* by Stephen King. One of them got a job at my answering service just so she could get my private number at home. She would call constantly, day and night, until someone would answer, then she would hang up. This went on for months. This was a real sick puppy.

But these distractions aside, I was feeling no pain during this time. Like I said, I was living in the eye of the hurricane. Self-centered, self-assured, the center of attention (but not centered), wild, wacky, impulsive, capricious, and impetuous. I must have been absolutely horrible to live with.

I didn't realize it at the time (unfortunately), but what I was going through was a sort of withdrawal: cold turkey from the addictive nature of the high-ballin' Monkee Express. The adulation, the attention, the power had wormed their way into my bloodstream as insidiously as any narcotic. I was going through the only phase of the up and down roller coaster ride of success that I *hadn't* had to go through after *Circus Boy*. Nothing had prepared me for the aftermath of something like the Monkees experience, and there really wasn't anything that could. Maybe I intuitively knew that the fall was going to come, and I was trying like hell to avoid it. But you can't avoid it. You *mustn't* avoid it. If you have the nerve, you should actually *use* the downward momentum to gather up speed, like a roller coaster, in order to get back on top. If only life were really as simple as a roller coaster.

Ten

Changes

Never had mortal man such opportunity,

Except Napoleon, or abused it more.

—George Gordon, Lord Byron
Don Juan

Even though Peter had officially quit the group, he fulfilled the rest of his obligations. One of these obligations was our first, and only, tour of the Far East. The tour went well enough, it was actually very successful, but you could feel the life blood of the Monkeemonster starting to ooze out . . . drip, drip, drip.

You gotta know that something's wrong when the highlight of your tour is landing in Tokyo and being told that you've received death threats from some fanatic Commie idiots who believe you epitomize the worst of American capitalistic corruption and greed. We had to have an armed police escort all the way from Narita Airport to our hotel. We stayed locked up in that hotel for days—being let out only to do the concerts, of course. I was scared to death. I had my roadies erect a massive contraption of cymbals around my drum set, and I hid behind them for the entire show. (As if that would have helped stop the slug from a high-powered rifle—a bit like the A-bomb drill in elementary school.)

Those Japanese concerts were very unusual, to say the least. In Japan, in those days, the audiences were still *very* formal. Screaming and yelling during the show was considered very bad manners! Instead, the girls expressed their rapture by waving little white handkerchiefs around in the air. After months of good ol' Western ear-splitting screams, this certainly took me by surprise. For the first time, I could actually hear the music we were making on stage, and I remember thinking, "this isn't that bad."

When Peter finally bid his last farewell, in December of 1968, Mike, Davy, and I continued to function as a trio for a while. We released two more albums, *Instant Replay* and *Monkees Present*. Though they did better than the soundtrack of *Head* had done, they still weren't anywhere as successful as the previous albums had been.

The good news was, I was stretching out as a songwriter. The bad news was that, though I was enjoying my creative freedom, the results were pretty weird. I wrote one very long song about my cat, "Shorty Blackwell," and another about how we had shafted the Indians, "Mommy and Daddy." These songs were full of personal meaning and creative integrity—and totally inaccessible.

Bob and Bert had all but abandoned the Monkees project after *Head* and were off producing movies with Jack Nicholson (*Easy Rider*). They had left us in the hands of very able-bodied delegates, like the associate producer Ward Sylvester, but they had essentially washed their hands of the whole affair. They did have one last laugh though—they got the three of us booked on *Hollywood Squares*. How embarrassing.

We also appeared on *The Glen Campbell Goodtime Hour*

and *The Johnny Cash Show*. These were good shows, but we were just kidding ourselves. We must have looked like a three-legged dog hobbling around. The snag was that, without the TV show as our foundation, we were floundering. The Monkees really didn't exist outside the auspices of the series, and we were kidding ourselves to think that they did. Without the PTB and the Magnificent Monkee Machine to guide and direct our activities, we started to wobble around like a top that's just about ready to fall over. Our next tour was probably the strangest tour anyone has ever done.

Mike and I were really into R&B at the time, and we decided that for our next concert tour we would use an all-black R&B band as our opening act *and* our backup band. Since Peter had quit there was no way we could play the music with just two instruments (Mike on guitar and me on drums), so I would come down off the drums and we would all stand together at the front of the stage kind of like Three Dog Monkee. We hired a R&B band that we'd seen at the good old Red Velvet nightclub called Sam and the Goodtimers. The results were laughable, if not ludicrous.

Don't get me wrong, Sam and the Goodtimers was a *great* R&B band. They would come out in matching black tuxedos and ruffled shirts, sit behind those little Lawrence Welk–type music stands, and play the shit out of Otis Redding, Sam Cooke, and Aretha Franklin songs. The only trouble was that *everything* they played tended to sound like Otis Redding, Sam Cooke, and Aretha Franklin. Consequently, when they backed us, all of *our* songs started sounding a bit like Otis Redding, Sam Cooke, and Aretha Franklin. You haven't lived until you've heard "I'm a Believer" sound like "Respect," or "I Wanna Be Free" sound like "Try a Little Tenderness." Unbelievable.

Needless to say, our fans must have thought we had finally lost our Monkee marbles. In a way, we had. The cancelled TV series was one lost marble, Peter quitting the group was another, the box office nonsuccess of *Head* and the *33⅓* fiasco were others, and straying from the PTB's original musical intention was yet another.

Mike, Davy, and I continued to play Monkees for a while, until Mike finally quit the group after I upstaged him one night on the Johnny Carson show. Then Davy and I kept the Monkees going for one album after that, *Changes,* and then finally . . . poof! That was it. No more Monkees.

It was really kind of funny if you think about it. Each successive album after *Pisces, Aquarius, Capricorn & Jones Ltd.* had begun to feature one less Monkee on the cover. First Peter had disappeared leaving only three, then Mike had vanished leaving two, then . . . nobody. It was like Michael J. Fox disappearing out of that photograph in *Back to the Future.*

There were no formal statements made. No explanations. No final farewell celebrations. No good-byes. Not even a traditional rock & roll fistfight to mark the final chapter.

The Monster Monkee Machine had simply fallen apart, slowly, bit by bit, little bit me by little bit you, until one day it wheezed its last wheeze, popped its last pop record, pulled over to the side of the road with its exhaust pipe dangling down . . . and just stopped.

In retrospect, it can be argued that if we'd have known what was good for us we would have just kept our mouths shut, sold zillions of albums, continued production on the tried and true TV series, and generally behaved like the good little Monkees that we were supposed to be.

It can also be argued that if we *had* continued doing the show, year after year, it might have become a very boring, predictable, worn-out old sitcom and might not enjoy the reputation it has today. After all, we made only fifty-six episodes of the show, and don't they say that good things come in small packages? Who knows what would have happened if Peter hadn't quit that day, if we had kept on recording, kept on filming, kept on Monkeeing around? It's a moot point. Maybe, somewhere in a parallel universe, there are four other versions of us, still living in that funky beach house, married, overweight, balding, bringing up teenage children who wear Reeboks and are into rap.

Cut to:

Int. Monkee Beach House—day—circa 2020

The four guys are sitting around the house. Mike is reading a copy of *Robocar and Driver*. Micky is watching *Star Trek* reruns on Virtual Holovision. Peter is mumbling to himself and tending to his hydroponic garden of brown rice. Davy is rubbing ointment on his hands.

MIKE
(*very slow drawl*)

Hey guys, did you see this new electric station wagon?

DAVY
(*rubbing furiously*)

Out damn liverspots!

PETER
(*incoherently*)

Mumble mumble . . . fat cat . . . mumble mumble . . . bourgeoisie pigs . . .

Suddenly, little MICKY JUNIOR comes running into the house with a bunch of his little friends.

MICKY JUNIOR

Dad . . . Hey, Dad! These guys don't believe me. Tell them the story about how you met Jimi Hendrix!

Micky smiles and takes off the virtual holovision goggles.

MICKY

All right, son. I'll tell you the story. But first, go get me that big box of Metamusil.

Fade Out

Anyway, I wasn't thinking about any of this at the time. I was just bopping around the Hollywood party scene, hanging out with Harry Nilsson and John Lennon during John's "Lost Weekend," and frankly just being a dilettante.

It wasn't long, though, before the reality of the situation caught up with me. I was sitting in the bath one day and had just washed my hair when I noticed that a *lot* of it had come out! I was completely unnerved. I look back on this moment as symbolic of what was happening to me at the time. I was literally falling to pieces.

Just like the other guys, I had deluded myself into thinking that I would be able to continue my career as a solo artist and maintain the same level of success that I had with the Monkees. Slowly, but surely, the truth became more and more self-evident; I had contracted that most dreaded of show business diseases: typecasting!

I signed up with a theatrical agent who tried his best to get me acting jobs. What he got back from the prospective casting agents and producers was, "Sorry, we don't need any *drummers.*" I couldn't believe it.

"But I'm an actor!" I retorted resentfully. "I was only playing the *part* of a drummer!" They couldn't, or wouldn't hear. I started to regret having used my real name on the show instead of a character name. To this day, I wonder if it would have made any difference to the success of the show; I know it certainly would have made a difference to my credibility as an actor.

I did manage to get considered for the role of Fonzie on *Happy Days,* but they gave the part to this new kid named Henry Winkler. (Henry has told me that he remembers seeing me at the interview and thinking, "Oh shit, Micky Dolenz is here, I'll never get the part!" I'm glad you did get it, Henry, you were great!) I also got a couple of guest shots on shows like *Adam-12* and *Cannon,* and did a couple of B movies; all in all not very exciting or lucrative endeavors.

I had similar problems in the recording arena as well. An old high school buddy of mine, Mike Curb, was running MGM records at the time and, to my everlasting gratitude, gave me a shot on the label. Unfortunately, the records I released disappeared without a trace. Harry Nilsson even produced me on one of his songs called "Daybreak," but I couldn't get any airplay. The stations, the distributors, the industry just wouldn't take me seriously. It was as if they were finally getting their revenge for having had the Monkees shoved down their throats for so long.

Fortunately, my mom had invested my money wisely and I was more or less solvent—I just couldn't get any serious work, as an actor, a musician, a singer, anything. I was going through that very same horrible period of rejection that my parents had so successfully saved me from after *Circus Boy.* That terrible why-don't-they-like-me-anymore? stage. It was dreadful. I definitely had a case of Leonard Nimoyitis. He even wrote a book about it called *I Am Not Spock.* Maybe I should have written one called *I Am Not Monkee.*

Obviously, I was not the first person to be caught in this typecasting trap, and I won't be the last. Unfortunately, it's kind of the curse that comes with the blessing. You work so hard to achieve success. You struggle to get to the top of the heap, and when you get there you discover that the very success you have attained has created this inertia that is subsequently almost impossible to overcome. Somebody should write a thesis about this.

Then, as if all this weren't enough, the greatest tragedy of my life hit me like a truck—Samantha divorced me.

I couldn't believe it; I was losing the wife and child I adored! I was devastated. I was furious. I wailed in protest and likened it to rats leaving a sinking ship. The truth is, I don't know how she stuck it out for as long as she did—the madness, the mayhem, the foolishness, the philandering, the late nights and listless days. One day she just decided she'd had enough; time to cut bait and run. Who could blame her?

There's a period of about a year in here (1975?) that is simply missing from my life. I was taking antidepressants, drinking a little too much, smoking a little too much, and completely wallowing in my self-made misery.

Harry Nilsson tells the story of how he called me up one night to see how I was doing. I must have sounded terrible because he came over immediately, only to find me sitting in the middle of the street, holding a half-empty bottle of Scotch, waiting to get hit by a car. (I must have still been in possession of some of my faculties because I did pick a street with *very* little traffic.) He brought me over to my friend Don Johnson's house, where I slept it off.

It took me a long time to get over the heartache of losing Samantha and Ami. Samantha and I are great friends now, but it took me a long time to recover from the trauma. (I'm not sure if one *ever* really recovers from that sort of blow.)

Fortunately, it was about this time that Tommy Boyce

and Bobby Hart came to me and asked if I wanted to go out on the road with them and Davy as Dolenz, Jones, Boyce and Hart—"the guys that sang 'em and the guys that wrote 'em." *The Monkees* had already been in reruns for a couple of years, and it seemed that there was some demand for us to tour again.

It came at the perfect time for me. I was drifting about quite aimlessly. I was spending some of my time watching TV, some of my time sleeping, and the rest of my time polishing the mouthpiece to my Luger.

We put together a show and hit the road. And we hit it hard: fair dates, club dates, lounge dates, amusement parks, the works. The five-star hotels and the airborne Monkee Express got traded in for Ramada Inns and a Buick station wagon. (Shades of Micky and the One-Nighters.)

But I was working and grateful for it. And we had a great time on that tour. Tommy and Bobby were wonderful to work with, and the audiences were very appreciative. We got a deal with Capitol Records and recorded a fine album called *Dolenz, Jones, Boyce & Hart.*

Things were looking up. I stopped the drinking, the smoking, the Valium, etc., and was beginning to get my life back in order.

A word about drugs. I have made no secret about the fact that I dabbled in the world of chemical realities. But, by most standards, I was pretty tame. And I was lucky. I'm not going to preach to anyone about the dangers of drug abuse, they should be self-evident. All I can tell you is that, in my experience, it simply wasn't worth it. It wasn't worth the money, the time, the energy, the damage to my physical and mental being, the damage to my relationships and my disposition. And, in the end, it also got so *boring.* My last experience with LSD was at a Malibu beach house in the company of Harry Nilsson, Brian Wilson, John Lennon, et al. With those participants, you'd think it would have been a stimulating, inspiring occasion. Unfortunately, it was not. Harry went off into his own world; Brian, who was already long-gone even at that time, played just one note on a piano, over and over again; and John stood and stared into a swimming pool for four hours. What fun! I ended up sitting in the living room, watching the walls breathe and my hand turn into a snake, impatiently looking at my watch thinking, "Here goes the old hand-into-a-snake routine. I wonder when I can get out of here and go home to work on my gyrocopter?"

(As an interesting side note; ever since I was a child, I've had a terrible habit of sniffing when I get nervous, or when my nose and throat get irritated by pollen, cigarette smoke, smog, etc. More than once I've had associates, and even close friends and family, ask me if I was on cocaine! I got so worried about getting such a reputation that I went to a hypnotherapist to try and break the habit. He had me lie on a couch and listen to soothing music. Now, when I get nervous, I don't sniff anymore, I just lie down wherever I am and go to sleep.)

But business was beginning to pick up. I started a small production company and began producing and directing some local commercials. A cameraman friend of mine named Allan Davio (who later became cinematographer on *E.T.* and *The Color Purple*) introduced me to a production manager named Stuart Gross. Stuart became my best friend and we remain very close to this day. Stuart encouraged me to develop my skills in the production end of the business and I did so, and I found I liked it a lot. In fact, I found I liked being behind the camera a lot more than I liked being in front of the camera. (And, if the truth be known, I still like it better.)

Believe it or not, I'm not sure that I was really cut out to be an entertainer. I certainly don't crave the attention; I never did. Although I'm very comfortable being in front of the camera, I can't say that I ever had a burning desire to perform. I often wonder what I would have chosen as my life's work if I had been left to my own devices. (At the time of the writing of this book, I am going back to school to study philosophy and quantum physics. I wonder what the hell *that* implies?)

But I took to behind-the-scenes production work like a lawyer to politics and started writing and developing TV shows and film scripts.

In the meantime, I was still working my "day job" as an ex-Monkee. Dolenz, Jones, Boyce & Hart were touring pretty steadily, and we eventually got booked on an extensive Far East tour. Like an idiot I went hang gliding two days before the tour and broke my arm! I did the entire tour with my arm in a sling and my brain on painkillers.

The D,J,B & H situation lasted for a few more months, and then Davy and I struck out on our own as Dolenz and Jones. Davy and I always worked well together on stage, and we continued to tour around the States dressed up in funny suits and singing the old songs over and over again. And over and over and over and . . .

But not being one to look a gift Monkee in the mouth, I stuck with it (even though the show was starting to look very much like a cheesy Vegas lounge act). Coco even came out with us on the road for a while and, thankfully, added a bit of class to the proceedings.

Davy and I did a musical in Sacramento based on *The Adventures of Tom Sawyer*. I played Huck Finn and Davy played Tom. (You haven't lived until you've heard Tom Sawyer with a thick North Country English accent.)

Then, somewhere along the line, William Morris, the big Hollywood talent agency, must have thought there was still some mileage left in the ol' Monkee machine, because one day Mike, Peter, Davy, and I actually ended up at my house to discuss an offer to do a McDonald's TV commercial. I remember the meeting well.

Cut To:

Int. Micky's House—Day

The four boys are pacing around the room, giving each other a wide berth. The atmosphere is electric. The mood is friendly but somewhat cautious, kindred but a tad defensive. Their shields are up. If they were dogs, they would all be pissing on the furniture.

They are all trying to pretend to each other how "successful" their mutual post-Monkee careers have been. The truth is, none of them has been very successful at all.

DAVY

So, what about this McDonald's thing?

MIKE
(*slow drawl*)

Well, I don't know, guys. You know I'm *really* busy these days.

DAVY
(*quickly*)

Oh yeah, me too. I'm *really, REALLY* busy these days.

MICKY

Right. Busy . . . Yeah, I'm *very* busy too. *Very* busy.

DAVY

What about you Peter?

PETER

If you think that I'm going to do a commercial for those meat-eating, fat cat, rain-forest-killing, bourgeoisie, fascist pigs . . .

Fade Out

Needless to say, we didn't do the commercial.

One day Harry Nilsson called me up and asked me if I wanted to costar along with Davy in the London production of his wonderful musical *The Point*. I immediately said yes. Little did I know that this decision would, once again, dramatically alter the course of my life. I started packing for my trip and looked forward with great anticipation to our Christmas opening at the celebrated Mermaid Theatre in the heart of London.

I arrived in England and settled into Harry Nilsson's flat in Mayfair, smack-dab in the middle of foggy London town. Harry had bought the luxurious flat some months before and frequently lent it out to his friends. (Harry eventually sold the flat when it became "jinxed." Tragically, both Mama Cass *and* Keith Moon died within its royal blue walls.)

But there was nothing negative about the flat or anything else when I moved in. London had meant a lot to me in the past, and I loved being back again.

It was a wonderful experience working at the Mermaid Theatre under the watchful eye of Sir Bernard Miles. Since I hadn't done a lot of theater at the time, I found it stimulating. I made some good friends during that time, like Colin Bennett, the actor and writer who would eventually work with me on a TV series called *Luna* starring a fourteen-year-old Patsy Kensit; and the wonderful choreographer Gillian Gregory, who had just done *Tommy* with the Who. Gillian and I would work together many times in the future, including *Bugsy Malone*, the London stage musical based on the Alan Parker movie.

I honestly thought that the run of *The Point* was going to be one of the highlights of my career. I thought that I would, finally, be able to break out of the mold that the Monkees had fashioned around me. Maybe, after this experience, I would be taken seriously. Davy and I would return to the States, continue our careers as singers, and I would be able to pursue my career as an actor. (Oh well, the best laid plans of mice and men.)

It was during this run of *The Point* that Davy and I had such a major falling out that we would not even speak to each other for nine years.

As I mentioned before, Davy had had his problems with managers, accountants, agents, business partners, etc. Let's face it, we all had had our problems at times. Unfortunately, I guess Davy had just let it get the better of him.

From my perspective, he was getting harder and harder to work with. He would always be late to meetings, rehearsals, shows; he would tend to be very suspicious of anybody new who would try to get close to him, and even more suspicious of any new deal that came his way. It seemed that he was determined to sabotage his own success. Somewhere along the line, and much to my dismay, he had changed from the fun-loving, cheeky little rascal I had known into an unhappy, bitter, misanthrope.

The atmosphere on *The Point* had started out clean and clear, but it gradually got thick and clouded with emotional pollution. Davy was drinking heavily and becoming unbearable to work with; and the cast and the director were coming to *me* as if I were my brother's keeper. They kept looking to me to sort him out as if I had some kind of mystical control over his actions. But I didn't know what to tell them. I suppose I should have tried harder to understand what was going on in his life that was twisting him up so badly. But, at that time, I wasn't the most stable person in the world either.

Anyway, one night after a performance, Davy and I had a

massive fight, a real knock-down, drag-out battle. We finished the play but I cancelled all of my upcoming engagements as Dolenz and Jones, and washed my hands of the entire relationship.

At that point, I was at a bit of a loss as to what to do. I had planned to go back to the States after the play and continue with the concerts, do some more acting, and pursue my career in production. Now I was footloose and fancy free. What to do? What to do?

The play in London had been booked for a limited run of twelve weeks over the holiday season, so I had only packed for a three-month trip. As it turned out, I stayed for fifteen years!

Eleven

Fast Forward

I don't want the cheese, I just want to

get out of the trap.

—Spanish proverb

Heav'n has no rage, like love to hatred turn'd,

Nor Hell a fury, like a woman scorn'd.

—William Congreve
The Mourning Bride

In the midway of this our mortal life,

I found me in a gloomy wood astray,

Gone from the path direct.

—Dante Alighieri
Inferno

They say everything happens for a reason. I suppose it can be argued that if I hadn't broken up with Samantha, if I hadn't accepted Harry's offer to do *The Point*, if I hadn't fallen out with Davy, if I hadn't decided to stay in jolly ol' England for a few months, my life would have taken a very different path back in 1975. As it turned out, the path it did take led me to some of the happiest and most fulfilling years of my life.

It was during the run of *The Point* that I was introduced to a wonderful literary agent named Linda Seifert (who still represents me in England to this day). I gave her my directing reel (as measly as it was at the time), and she offered to banter my name around town to see if anyone was interested in me as a director. I was not optimistic. I had only a couple of commercials and one episode of *The Monkees* on my reel and, being the realist that I am, I knew it would hardly be enough to launch a directorial career.

Fortunately for me, the BBC had just started producing a series called *Premiere*, the purpose of which was to introduce new, first-time drama directors to British television. Talk about coincidence. I met with its producer, a very bright man named Graham Benson and, much to my surprise, he offered me one of the episodes to direct. I was thrilled.

The filming went very well. The experience convinced me beyond a doubt that directing was indeed the direction I wanted to take with my professional life, and I poured my heart and soul into my newfound career.

Soon after the BBC assignment, I started going on interviews for other directing chores, and within a few months I got an offer to produce and direct a series for London Weekend Television. My mentor at LWT was a wonderful producer named Humphrey Barclay. The name of the show was *Metal Mickey* (another coincidence). It was a sitcom starring Irene Handl about a kid who builds a robot in his basement and it suddenly comes alive (the robot, not the basement). The series was very successful and ran for a number of years. It also firmly established me as a bona fide programmaker. It was also at this time that I officially changed my name to "Michael" Dolenz. I did so for a couple of reasons: (1) I felt that "Michael" was a more formal name to go along with my newly acquired executive status, and (2) the robot Metal Mickey was quite sophisticated, and when we were rehearsing and someone would say "Micky," we would *both* turn around!

The truth was that I did feel like a new person. I found that the British don't have nearly the same problem with typecasting as they do here in the States. Providing that I could prove that I knew what I was doing, the industry was quite happy to accept me as a director, and I was soon working full-time. And, best of all, there was no mention made of the Monkees . . . ever.

Notwithstanding that I was separated from Ami by the Atlantic Ocean and the American continent, these were some of the best days of my life. I had broken the mold! Typecasting be damned! Long live the Queen! I began to build myself quite an impressive career in the distinguished British television industry.

Aside from the long run of *Metal Mickey*, I worked on a number of TV shows and short films. One of the films, *The Box*, was written by two of the members of Monty Pythons' Flying Circus, Michael Palin and Terry Jones.

I shot dozens of commercials and music videos starring the likes of Leonard Rossiter and discovered a very funny, talented young actor named Robbie Coltrane, who I cast in a film version of the old Peter Sellers hit record *Badham, Gateway to the South*. David Putnam was the executive producer on that one.

I bought the rights to the American series *Fernwood Tonight* and produced a British version written by Ruby Wax for English television.

I bought the stage production rights to Alan Parker's wonderful movie *Bugsy Malone*, wrote the stage version, and directed it at Her Majesty's Theatre in London.

One day I got a call from none other than Mike Nesmith, who asked me to direct a couple of segments for his TV series *Television Parts*. I did so gladly, and elicited the services of some contemporary British comedy greats like Rik Mayall, Ade Edmondson, Mel Smith, Griff Rhys Jones, Alexie Sayle, and the entire cast of *Spitting Image*. I thought Mike's series was great, and I was sorry to see that it wasn't picked up.

As if all that wasn't enough to keep me busy, I produced and directed that wonderful British funny man Bill Oddie in a series he created called *From the Top*.

My personal life had also taken a turn for the better. I really jumped into the English thing with both feet. I joined a "proper" London men's sporting club where you had to wear a coat and tie to play squash. I got married again and had three of the most gorgeous children the world has ever known—three little girls: Charlotte, Emily, and Georgia Dolenz. At the time of this writing they are eleven, nine, and eight, respectively, and they are the lights of my life. Imagine the thrill of having three little action-packed princesses jumping up and down on your head while you're taking a nap on a Sunday afternoon.

My career as a producer/director kept flourishing in the eighties, and I was soon able to pick and choose what I wanted to do. I started developing and producing shows of my own creation, like *Luna* starring a very young, beautiful actress named Patsy Kensit. This was a series about a little girl who lives in the future. Kind of a cross between Terry Gilliam's *Brazil* and *The Jetsons.* I had come up with the original concept way back in the late sixties, and the character was modeled on my ruminations of what it might be like for Ami growing up in the future.

I made some very good friends in England, like the marvellous actor Robin Askwith. They say that the English are stuffy and unapproachable; I found this not to be true at all. There is, however, a sense of social propriety that does tend to keep people at a distance. I don't think this is such a bad thing. The contrary is true, of course, in the States, and especially in Los Angeles. Here, it is not uncommon for a new acquaintance to immediately treat you like a lifelong friend and start telling you about his latest hemorrhoid operation. I rather like the English habit of slowly developing a friendship along more settled lines. In my opinion, it certainly does make for better and more long-lasting affiliations. I noticed the same behavior in Japan, also an island culture. It must come from the need for privacy. I suppose that on a small island, crowded with people, if you didn't have certain social customs like this you would very soon get on each other's nerves and kill each other off.

Then, one day in 1986, I got a call from none other than Peter Tork! He said that he had been approached by a tour producer in New York named David Fishof who wanted to put the Monkees back on the road to celebrate the twentieth anniversary of the TV show. The money wasn't very good, and I declined the offer. I was due to start production on a new television series and, quite frankly, I had no desire to get back on stage again. I was very happy working behind the scenes, living with my beautiful little girls in our seventeen-room Georgian home deep in the English countryside, riding my great big Irish hunters, playing polo, driving my new Jaguar convertible, and generally living the life of an English country gentleman. Why should I want to disappear off to the States and tour around singing old songs?

David Fishof raised the offer. I declined again. He raised the offer again. Suddenly, I had a great idea! Why not take the kids on tour with me and show them the States from the windows of a Rock & Roll tour bus!

Then, David Fishof raised the offer again, and between the raised offers and the prospect of "gigging" with my three little angels in tow, I agreed to hit the road.

So I managed to get out of my contract for the TV series, I packed up the three little girls, closed up the country house, and set out for what was to be a brief, twelve-week reunion tour with the guys from the old group.

Just like my situation with *The Point*, I originally intended to be on the road for just that one summer (1986). Three years later, I was still on the road, up to my butt in chili dogs, and Davy and I were once again at each other's throat.

There's no business like show business.

Mike Nesmith had declined to get back together with the three of us for the tour, so Davy, Peter, and I met up one day at a resort in the Catskill mountains to start rehearsing for the show. I had spoken to Peter over the phone but hadn't actually spoken to Davy at all. I had insisted that we each negotiate our contracts individually.

As the start of the tour drew closer, I found myself getting very excited about the new venture. I had discovered that MTV was rerunning *The Monkees* regularly and, thanks to them, it seemed that we had a whole new generation of fans to support us. It would make a nice break for the family, and it would give me a chance to get out of the television studio for a while and play at being a "rock star" again.

I was slightly apprehensive about how Davy and I would get along, but I figured it *had* been nine years since we had had any contact and surely he *must* have buried the hatchet by now and forgotten the past. I was wrong.

Davy showed up on the very first day with his hackles up, his tail feathers sticking straight out, and immediately started to stake out his territory. He'd even brought along this silly little English guy who was supposedly his "bodyguard." It was all I could do to keep from bursting out laughing. But Davy wasn't laughing. He took to insulting me whenever he could and generally making things very uncomfortable. I couldn't believe it. It was like he was still living in the past. Harboring old animosities and insecurities.

But I managed to grin and bear it. We started rehearsing, and Peter and I graciously allowed Davy to "stage" the show to indulge his ego. (Staging the show basically consisted of compiling a song list.)

I'm pretty good at disarming antagonistic people, and soon Davy realized that I was not threatening him, and his anxieties subsided. We even started having some fun! But it was not to last for long. Arista Records offered us the record deal and things quickly started to fall apart. You can review the results of that incident by turning back to Chapter One.

Like the old saying goes, "What started out as a day of enjoyment—ended in tragedy." Though the tour was very successful financially, the emotional and psychological anxiety made it a bitter success for me. The tension between Davy, Peter, and me became unpalatable, and to make matters worse, we were being sued, slagged off, and snubbed by some of the most important PTB in the business at the time. Here I had been living the life of a respected television producer and director and suddenly I was being regarded as a nefarious troublemaker. "What is wrong with this picture?" I kept asking myself. With all the stress of dealing with the crumbling Monkee business, and living on the road out of suitcases and cardboard boxes, my "sniff-rate" went up a thousand percent and I became very ill, both mentally and physically. I didn't recover for months.

It can be argued that I still haven't.

So here I am. It's 1993, and to say that I am at a crossroads in my life would be a gross understatement.

At times I feel like I'm actually standing in a crossroads with a couple of ten-ton trucks coming from both directions.

I'm trying to start up a new career in the States after being gone for fifteen years, but so what? No one said it would be easy.

I'm pushing fifty, but so what? Age only matters if you're cheese.

The good news is: Now that I'm back in L.A. I'm spending a lot of time with Ami (who has become a very successful actress). Samantha and I have become good friends. Stuart Gross and I are hanging out together again, playing polo, and my new manager/friend Kevin Allyn and his wife Robyn are supporting my every endeavor.

The roller coaster is approaching a big hill and is slowing down a bit; it's going to be a long, sluggish ride to the top, but the top will come—I have no doubt of that. And, when it does, I'll be ready. I'll raise up my hands, close my eyes, and . . . *wheeeee!*

The stupid fear fortune, the wise endure it.

—Roman Proverb

Micky Dolenz and The Monkees—Into the Twenty-First Century

In the eleven years since this book was first published, there have been an unprecedented number of new events, recordings, concert tours, and television appearances in the life of Micky Dolenz. Appearing both solo and with his famous Monkees compatriots—Davy Jones, Peter Tork, and Mike Nesmith—his career continues to evolve and blossom. The many highlights have included the release of the first all-new Monkees studio album in 28 years, a new network television special, and a made-for-TV movie about their phenomenal career together. There have also been several fresh Monkees CD packages on the marketplace, including previously unreleased material, a twenty-first-century live concert album, and the emergence of several Monkees projects on DVD. Micky has also launched several high profile solo projects—as an actor, a director, and as the voice of several cartoon characters. In 2003 he took the solo spotlight and starred in the touring company of the Broadway show *Aida*. And in 2004 he made his official Broadway debut when he joined the Manhattan cast of that same show.

This new and highly active phase of Dolenz' career began in the early 1990s, when Micky released two solo children's albums. The first one was entitled *Micky Dolenz Puts You to Sleep* (1993). It was a collection of '60s pop tunes presented as lullabies. In 1994 Micky released a sequel to it called *Broadway Micky*. It featured the same lullaby-styled arrangements and was also released by the children's division of Rhino Records (Kid Rhino).

That same year Micky provided the voice of the animated character Arthur the Moth on the first season of the FOX cartoon series *The Tick*. In addition, Dolenz replaced Davy Jones as DJ Vince Fontaine in the Off-Broadway production of *the* hit show *Grease!* And, later that year, he and Davy teamed up to launch a series of Monkees duet concert performances in the United States.

In November of 1994, fans of the group and their circle were shocked by the news of songwriter Tommy Boyce's sudden death. Boyce, who was 55 at the time, committed suicide in his Nashville home. Over the past couple of years he had moved to Tennessee, where he maintained homes in Memphis and Nashville. He was frequently seen as a performer at songwriter's showcases at the famed Bluebird Café in Nashville, introducing audiences to his newest material. Best known for having penned the trademark Monkees theme, "Hey, Hey, We're The Monkees" and "(I'm Not Your) Stepping Stone," with partner Bobby Hart, Tommy's death saddened fans around the world.

In 1994 and 1995, in an elaborate campaign, Rhino Records reissued every one of the original Monkees' studio albums. The albums were released in nonsequential order, each remastered for improved sound, and all containing special bonus tracks. These bonus tracks included alternate versions of previously released Monkees songs, as well as never-before-released Monkees songs, alternate mixes, and demo recordings. Three of the albums—*Instant Replay*; *The Monkees Present: Micky, David, Michael*; and *Changes*—had never been on CD before that time.

In 1995 Micky joined his Monkees partners Peter and Davy to guest star on a popular Pizza Hut TV commercial. Known as the "Wrong Way" series of Pizza Hut ads, the trio of Monkees costarred in the commercial with Beatle Ringo Starr.

In March of 1996, Rhino Records released the Monkees' CD *Missing Links, Volume 3.* Like its two predecessors, this album featured 18 rare and never-before-released songs, demos, and rare takes of several Monkees' recordings. Amongst the songs included on it is a version of *The Monkees* TV show theme sung in Italian, a Kellogg's cereal jingle, a new mix of "Circle Sky," the single version of "She Hangs Out," Micky's psychedelic-sounding "You're No Good," Peter's "Merry Go Round," and a version of Neil Diamond's "Love to Love."

Three of the most exciting Dolenz tracks included on *Missing Links, Volume 3* are "Midnight Train," "She'll Be There," and "Shake 'Em Up," all recorded with his sister Coco providing harmony vocals. The first two tracks were originally produced by Chip Douglas in 1967 for the *Headquarters* album, which never made the final release. According to Micky, he has always loved singing with his little sister: "We always had a great blend. We started singing together the day she was born!"

Reviewed in *Record Collector* magazine, writer Peter Doggett proclaimed that *Missing Links, Volume 3* was, "A wonderful mix of out-takes, radio jingles and rarities . . . this is the way archive releases should sound." That same year, Rhino released a new single disc, 20-track CD called *Monkees Greatest Hits.* It traced the group's career up to and including "Heart and Soul" from the *Pool It* album.

The year 1996 found Micky doing several solo appearances on American TV shows. He guest starred as the Mayor in USA's *Pacific Blue.* And he was seen on the popular shows *Boy Meets World, Politically Incorrect,* and *Muppets Tonight.*

From June to August of 1996 the most incredible thing happened—all four of the original Monkees got together in NRG Recording Studios in North Hollywood to create their first new album as a quartet in three decades! Released in the fall of '96, the resulting Rhino album, entitled *Justus*, was truly the fulfillment of a dream for Micky, Peter, Mike, and Davy. After years of having recorded other people's material with studio musicians and outside producers, the famed quartet finally created an album written by them, sung by them, with music played and produced by them. Of the 12 songs on the album, Micky Dolenz penned five songs, and shared writing credit with Davy Jones on a sixth song—the touching "You and I." Davy, Peter and Mike each wrote two songs apiece for the album.

Unlike in the past, when Mike Nesmith routinely declined being part of Monkees tours and Monkees albums, this time around he was the driving force behind the project. Recording *Justus* was his idea, and everyone gladly joined the project.

Mike followed his signature country/rock stylings on his update of "Circle Sky." Davy presented several sentimental ballads. The finest is his heartfelt composition "It's Not Too Late." And Peter is especially brilliant on the jazzy and introspectively poetic "I Believe You."

Micky's solo songs were amongst the most impressive cuts on the album. They included the self-empowering ballad "It's My Life"; the pointed social commentary about life in suburbia, "Regional Girl"; and the rocking lament of love-gone-wrong entitled "Never Enough."

Justus was truly a joint effort by the quartet. According to Peter Tork, the minute the quartet all got into the recording studio together, they instantly clicked musically. There was no awkwardness and no personal baggage. "We just turned up our amps, played as loud as we wanted, and it was right there. There were no problems. It was as good as it ever was," he claimed.

Davy found the *Justus* recording process to be the most liberating experience of all of their albums: "It's just the four of us playing now, so nobody's going to be saying, 'They can't do this. They can't do that.'" Instead, they did it all and they did it their way!

When this exciting new album came together so seamlessly, no one was more happily surprised than Micky. He claimed, "I never thought in a million years that this could happen again. I want to thank Papa Naz [Nesmith] for his vision, support, patience, and encouragement. For my money, he single-handedly made this album possible."

The group received a lot of favorable press at the time of the release of the *Justus* album. They also received some great reviews. One of the most glowing ones came from Carl Cafarelli in *Goldmine* magazine. According to him, "It's Dolenz who really shines as lead singer on six of the album's 12 tracks . . . Dolenz sings here from the broken heart and the wounded soul, possessed of a passion we've not heard from him in ages, and spitting out a vitriolic anger we've never heard from da Mickster. Forget about the oldies tours; here, Dolenz reminds us of why he's simply one of the best (and certainly the most consistently underrated) rock 'n' roll singers on record. And his drumming is superbly forceful and authoritative throughout *Justus*."

To support the release of the *Justus* album, the quartet of Micky, Davy, Peter, AND Mike performed an exciting live show at the Billboard Live Club in Los Angeles. Having a great time together as a foursome, the touring continued in 1997 for a month-long tour of the U.K. in March.

The release of the *Justus* album and the British tour were just the start of a year of multimedia events for the group.

On January 22, 1997, the cable TV network The Disney Channel aired a documentary called *Hey, Hey, We're The Monkees*. Interviews with all four members of the group made this a fascinating look back at the career of the group, and encompassed all of the new and concurrent projects in which they were involved.

On February 17, 1997, ABC-TV presented a brand new hour-long reunion of The Monkees. Entitled *Hey, Hey, It's The Monkees*, the special found the group back in character, in the same beach-house mode that TV audiences remembered from the 1960s. Explained Micky at the time, "We're doing this show as if The Monkees had gone through all the changes four men would go through over the past 30 years." According to him, the script of the new show had more of an updated feeling to it: "It's gotten more intelligent, maybe a little wittier. We're not trying to be zany, and we're not trying."

One of the most exciting aspects of the TV special was that all four of The Monkees were united in front of the cameras for the first time since they filmed *Head* and *33⅓ Revolutions Per Monkee* in the 60s. Explained Mike, "We look back on those records and those television shows with a lot of pride and think, 'Gee, that was great, and we had a great time doing that.' And I still want to do that. That's why I don't want to go back and try to revisit it like a high school reunion, I just want to keep on going. And that's what the [TV special] script does to a great degree. It's like we just never quit."

On April 21, 1997, VH1 tipped off still another group TV show revival, when they ran back-to-back episodes of *The Monkees* all day long. Following that marathon, the television network commenced airing episodes of the half-hour series every Saturday at 10:00 a.m.—similar to what had been successfully done in the 1970s. Throughout the summer and fall of 1997, the trio of Micky, Davy, and Peter toured the United States in concert. For this tour Dolenz divided his stage time between his famous drum kit, playing guitar, and singing his many lead vocals.

In 1998, Rhino Records released a great two-disc CD retrospective package by the group, with a distinctive 3D cover, entitled *The Monkees Anthology*. This album is the first hits package to span the group's music from the '60s to the '90s, by including "You and I" from the *Justus* album.

Meanwhile, Micky kept busy with his own solo projects. He went to the other side of the TV cameras that year to direct an episode of the popular ABC-TV series *Boy Meets World*. Micky's fans also got to hear his versatile voice as two of the canine characters on the Fox network cartoon show *The Secret Files of the SpyDogs*. He provided the voice for Ralph, the leader of the SpyDogs, and for Scrabble, the puppy who is a SpyDog in training.

The years 2000 and 2001 found Micky touring the U.S. as one of the headliners of the all-star Teen Idols concert tour. During this era he also performed in concert as a solo act, and for several dates he performed as a duet with his sister Coco.

The Monkees joined the DVD era on June 12, 2000, when Rhino Records released the group's first two packages in the new video format. The first one was entitled *Our Favorite Episodes*. It found each of the group members naming his most memorable half hour of their famed TV series, and these four shows were presented together in one package. Davy's favorite episode was "Royal Flush," Peter selected "Monkee vs. Machine," Mike chose "Fairy Tale," and Micky's pick was the series finale episode "Mijacogeo (The Frodis Caper)." At the same time, The Monkees' legendary and much-misunderstood movie, *Head*, was also released on DVD.

After being bantered about for years, finally, in the year 2000, VH1 released a biographical film based on the phenomenal career of The Monkees. With actors portraying Micky, Mike, Peter, and Davy, the made-for-TV movie was entitled *Daydream Believers: The Monkees Story*. The production received mixed reviews, but everyone seemed to agree that the film accurately portrayed much of the excitement, the adventure, the drugs, and the rock & roll that the group's heyday had encompassed.

In 2001, Rhino Records replaced its popular and well-received 4-CD boxed set, *Listen to the Band*, with a newly re-mastered 4-CD retrospective. Entitled *Music Box*, this package was physically in the style of a cardboard-bound booklet, as opposed to the '90s "candy box" set with its over-sized book contained within. It covered much of the same musical material, and the same span of recordings—from the '60s to the '80s—expanding its scope by adding two cuts from 1996's *Justus*.

That same year, Micky, Peter, and Davy went back out on tour as a Monkees trio. It was their first tour together in a couple of years, and while they were on the road they recorded a new concert album and a DVD. Both 2003 releases, entitled *Live Summer Tour*, were taken from their performance at The Sun Theater in Anaheim, California, on August 31, 2001.

The summer of 2002 found the group back on the concert road again. For this tour, The Monkees were once again the duo of Micky Dolenz and Davy Jones. Touring with a backup band, Dolenz and Jones took turns singing their individually led hits, and vocally backing each other up. Their series of concert dates included a stop at Hollywood's famed House of Blues rock nightclub on Sunset Strip. For that particular gig, the stage was warmed up by another TV singing star, Barry Williams, who played the role of Greg on *The Brady Bunch*.

On September 20, 2002, Micky married his longtime girlfriend, Donna Quinter. They had met in the early '90s. Actually, it was New York City disc jockey Jim Kerr who had originally introduced the two of them to each other. For many years they kept up a long distance relationship;

Donna's job working for a major airline kept her as busy as Micky's own hectic schedule occupied him. Finally, after the events of 9/11, Micky drove across country to get Donna out of New York and on the way back to Los Angeles he surprised her with a marriage proposal. According to Micky, he has never been happier. "I am thrilled, it's wonderful," he proclaims.

During this era, two more compilations of single-disc Monkees' "greatest hits" were released. They include 2002's 12-cut *The Essentials: The Monkees*, and 2003's more deluxe 25-song *The Best of The Monkees*. The later CD features a special five-song bonus Karaoke disc, so that one can live out their own lifelong ambition of actually singing like a Monkee.

The most exciting Monkees reissue came in 2003 in the form of two deluxe multi-DVD packages of every TV episode of *The Monkees*. Presented as *The Complete First Season* and *The Complete Second Season*, these Rhino DVD compilations represent ultimate video collections for the true Monkees collector.

In the year 2003, Micky Dolenz was busy starring in the touring company of the hit Broadway show *Aida*. Based on the classic opera of the same name, this production of *Aida* has all new music penned by Elton John and Tim Rice. Dolenz portrayed the role of Zoser, the show's prime villain, and he performed two songs. Then, in January of 2004, Micky made his Broadway debut as part of the New York City cast of *Aida*. After 40-plus years as a TV star (in both *Circus Boy* and *The Monkees*) and as a rock star, Micky Dolenz was finally a bona fide Broadway star!

Meanwhile, the other members of The Monkees have also been busy pursuing their own solo projects as well. Peter Tork regularly appears in Los Angeles clubs with his new blues band, Shoe Suede Blues. Davy Jones performs solo with his own rock band, and in 2003 he was seen as the host

of a cable TV show about the royal families of Europe. And
Mike Nesmith is still recording his own solo material.

Just as with most of their five-decade careers together
and apart, one never knows when the next Monkees revival
is due to hit, and which configuration of the foursome it will
include. As long as there are fans out there to appreciate
their music, their performing, and their long and illustrious
careers, the legend of The Monkees and Micky Dolenz will
continue to grow. Fortunately for all of us, there is undoubtedly much more Monkees magic to come!

Mark Bego, 2004

Discography

Albums:

NOTE: The following sales figures are for the United States only, although albums were released in over 20 different countries around the world. Total sales of Monkees are in excess of 70 million worldwide.

*****Quintuple Platinum for sales in excess of 5 million copies
***Triple Platinum for sales in excess of 3 million
*Platinum for sales in excess of 1 million
+Gold for sales in excess of 500,000

In the 1990s each of the original nine non-Greatest Hits albums were remastered and rereleased by Rhino Records on CD, each containing "Bonus Tracks" not found on the original vinyl and CD albums. Those additional songs are individually identified as being a "Bonus Track."

with The Monkees

(1) *The Monkees*
(Colgems Records / 1966)
[Number One Chart Hit / 13 Weeks]*****
(Rhino Records—Extended Version / 1994)
    1. "(Theme from) *The Monkees*"
    2. "Saturday's Child"
    3. "I Wanna Be Free"
    4. "Tomorrow's Gonna Be Another Day"

5. "Papa Gene's Blues"
6. "Take a Giant Step"
7. "Last Train to Clarksville"
8. "This Just Doesn't Seem to Be My Day"
9. "Let's Dance On"
10. "I'll Be True to You"
11. "Sweet Young Thing"
12. "Gonna Buy Me a Dog"
13. "I Can't Get Her off My Mind" Bonus Track / Previously Unreleased Version
14. "I Don't Think You Know Me" Bonus Track / Previously Unreleased Version
15. "(Theme from) *The Monkees*" Bonus Track / Previously Unreleased Version

(2) *More of The Monkees*
(Colgems Records / 1967)
[Number One Chart Hit / 18 Weeks]*****
(Rhino Records—Extended Version / 1994)
1. "She"
2. "When Love Comes Knockin' (At Your Door)"
3. "Mary, Mary"
4. "Hold on Girl"
5. "Your Auntie Grizelda"
6. "(I'm Not Your) Steppin' Stone"
7. "Look Out (Here Comes Tomorrow)"
8. "The Kind of Girl I Could Love"
9. "The Day We Fall in Love"
10. "Sometime in the Morning"
11. "Laugh"
12. "I'm a Believer"
13. "Don't Listen to Linda" Bonus Track
14. "I'll Spend My Life with You" Bonus Track / Alternate Version
15. "I Don't Think You Know Me" Bonus Track / Previously Unreleased

16. "Look Out (Here Comes Tomorrow)" Bonus Track / Alternate Version
17. "I'm a Believer" Bonus Track / Alternate Version

(3) *Headquarters*
(Colgems Records / 1967)
[Number One Chart Hit / One Week]***
(Rhino Records—Extended Version / 1995)
1. "You Told Me"
2. "I'll Spend My Life with You"
3. "Forget That Girl"
4. "Band 6"
5. "You Just May Be the One"
6. "Shades of Gray"
7. "I Can't Get Her off My Mind"
8. "For Pete's Sake"
9. "Mr. Webster"
10. "Sunny Girlfriend"
11. "Zilch"
12. "No Time"
13. "Early Morning Blues and Greens"
14. "Randy Scouse Git"
15. "All of Your Toys" Bonus Track / Alternate Version
16. "The Girl I Knew Somewhere" Bonus Track / Alternate Version
17. "Peter Gunn's Gun" Bonus Track
18. "Jericho" Bonus Track
19. "Nine Times Blue" Bonus Track / Demo Version
20. "Pillow Time" Bonus Track / Demo Version

(4) *Pisces, Aquarius, Capricorn & Jones Ltd.*
(Colgems Records / 1967)
[Number One / Five Weeks]***
(Rhino Records—Extended Version / 1995)
1. "Salesman"
2. "She Hangs Out"

3. "The Door Into Summer"
4. "Love Is Only Sleeping"
5. "Cuddly Toy"
6. "Words"
7. "Hard to Believe"
8. "What Am I Doing Hangin' 'Round?"
9. "Peter Percival Patterson's Pet Pig Porky"
10. "Pleasant Valley Sunday"
11. "Daily Nightly"
12. "Don't Call on Me"
13. "Star Collector"
14. "Special Announcement" Bonus Track / Previously Unreleased Version
15. "Goin' Down" Bonus Track / Previously Unreleased Alternate Mix
16. "Salesman" Bonus Track / Previously Unreleased Alternate Mix
17. "The Door Into Summer" Bonus Track / Previously Unreleased Alternate Mix
18. "Love Is Only Sleeping" Bonus Track / Previously Unreleased Alternate Mix
19. "Daily Nightly" Bonus Track / Previously Unreleased Alternate Mix
20. "Star Collector" Bonus Track / Previously Unreleased Alternate Mix

(5) *The Birds, The Bees, and The Monkees*
(Colgems Records / 1968)
[Number Three]*
(Rhino Records—Extended Version / 1994)

1. "Dream World"
2. "Auntie's Municipal Court"
3. "We Were Made for Each Other"
4. "Tapioca Tundra"
5. "Daydream Believer"
6. "Writing Wrongs"
7. "I'll Be Back up on My Feet"

8. "The Poster"
9. "P.O. Box 9847"
10. "Magnolia Simms"
11. "Valleri"
12. "Zor and Zam"
13. "Alvin" Bonus Track / Previously Unreleased Alternate Mix
14. "I'm Gonna Try" Bonus Track / Previously Unreleased
15. "P.O. Box 9847" Bonus Track / Previously Unreleased Alternate Mix
16. "The Girl I Left behind Me" Bonus Track / Previously Unreleased Alternate Version
17. "Lady's Baby" Bonus Track / Previously Unreleased Alternate Version

(6) *Head* [Original Soundtrack Album]
(Colgems Records / 1968)
[Number 45]
(Rhino Records—Extended Version / 1994)
1. "Opening Ceremony"
2. "Porpoise Song (Theme from *Head*)"
3. "Ditty Diego—War Chant"
4. "Circle Sky"
5. "Supplicio"
6. "Can You Dig It?"
7. "Gravy"
8. "Superstitious"
9. "As We Go Along"
10. "Dandruff?"
11. "Daddy's Song"
12. "Poll"
13. "Long Title: Do I Have to Do This All over Again"
14. "Swami—Plus Strings"
15. "Ditty Diego—War Chant" Bonus Track / Alternate Version
16. "Circle Sky" Bonus Track / Alternate Version
17. "Happy Birthday to You" Bonus Track

18. "Can You Dig It?" Bonus Track / Long Version
19. "Daddy's Song" Bonus Track / Alternate Version
20. "*Head* Radio Spot" Bonus Track

(7) *Instant Replay*
(Colgems Records / 1969)
[Number 32]
(Rhino Records—Extended Version / 1995)

1. "Through the Looking Glass"
2. "Don't Listen to Linda"
3. "I Won't Be the Same without Her"
4. "Just a Game"
5. "Me without You"
6. "Don't Wait for Me"
7. "You and I"
8. "While I Cry"
9. "Teardrop City"
10. "The Girl I Left behind Me"
11. "A Man without a Dream"
12. "Shorty Blackwell"
13. "Someday Man" Bonus Track
14. "Carlisle Wheeling" Bonus Track / Previously Unreleased Alternate Version
15. "Rosemarie" Bonus Track / Previously Unreleased Early Version
16. "Smile" Bonus Track / Previously Unreleased Version
17. "St. Matthew" Bonus Track / Previously Unreleased Alternate Mix
18. "Me without You" Bonus Track / Previously Unreleased Alternate Mix
19. "Through the Looking Glass" Bonus Track / Previously Unreleased Alternate Mix

(8) *The Monkees Greatest Hits* [Vinyl Only]
(Colgems Records / 1969)
[Number 98]

1. "Daydream Believer"
2. "Pleasant Valley Sunday"

3. "Cuddly Toy"
4. "Shades of Gray"
5. "Zor or Zam"
6. "A Little Bit Me, A Little Bit You"
7. "She"
8. "Randy Scouse Git"
9. "I Wanna Be Free"
10. "I'm a Believer"
11. "Valleri"
12. "Mary, Mary"
13. "(I'm Not Your) Steppin' Stone"
14. "Last Train to Clarksville"

(9) *The Monkees Present: Micky, David, Michael*
(Colgems Records / 1969)
[Number 100]
(Rhino Records—Extended Version / 1994)

1. "Little Girl"
2. "Good Clean Fun"
3. "If I Knew"
4. "Bye Bye Baby Bye Bye"
5. "Never Tell a Woman Yes"
6. "Looking for the Good Times"
7. "Ladies Aid Society"
8. "Listen to the Band"
9. "French Song"
10. "Mommy and Daddy"
11. "Oklahoma Backroom Dancer"
12. "Pillow Time"
13. "Calico Girlfriend Samba" Bonus Track / Previously Unreleased
14. "The Good Earth" Bonus Track / Previously Unreleased
15. "Listen to the Band" Bonus Track / Previously Unreleased
16. "Mommy and Daddy" Bonus Track / Previously Unreleased
17. "*The Monkees Present* Radio Promo" Bonus Track / Previously Unreleased

(10) *Changes*
(Colgems / 1970)
(Rhino Records—Extended Version / 1994)
1. "Oh My My"
2. "Ticket on a Ferry Ride"
3. "You're So Good to Me"
4. "It's Got to Be Love"
5. "Acapulco Sun"
6. "99 Pounds"
7. "Tell Me Love"
8. "Do You Feel It Too?"
9. "I Love You Better"
10. "All Alone in the Dark"
11. "Midnight Train"
12. "I Never Thought It Peculiar"
13. "Time and Time Again" Bonus Track
14. "Do It in the Name of Love" Bonus Track
15. "Lady Jane" Bonus Track

(11) *Monkees Greatest Hits* [New Version]
(Arista Records / 1976)
[Number 58]+
1. "(Theme from) *The Monkees*"
2. "Last Train to Clarksville"
3. "She"
4. "Daydream Believer"
5. "Listen to the Band"
6. "A Little Bit Me, A Little Bit You"
7. "I'm a Believer"
8. "I Wanna Be Free"
9. "Pleasant Valley Sunday"
10. "(I'm Not Your) Steppin' Stone"
11. "Shades of Gray"

(12) *More Greatest Hits of The Monkees*
(Arista Records / 1982)
1. "Take a Giant Step"
2. "Mary, Mary"

3. "Sometime in the Morning"
4. "Cuddly Toy"
5. "Randy Scouse Git"
6. "Words"
7. "Valleri"
8. "You Just May Be the One"
9. "The Girl I Knew Somewhere"
10. "Saturday's Child"
11. "Look Out (Here Comes Tomorrow"
12. "For Pete's Sake (Closing Theme)"

(13) *Then & Now . . . The Best of The Monkees*
(Arista Records / 1986)
[Number 20]+

1. "(Theme from) *The Monkees*"
2. "Last Train to Clarksville"
3. "Take a Giant Step"
4. "(I'm Not Your) Steppin' Stone"
5. "She"
6. "A Little Bit Me, A Little Bit You"
7. "I'm a Believer"
8. "Look Out (Here Comes Tomorrow)"
9. "Sometime in the Morning"
10. "The Girl That I Knew Somewhere"
11. "Randy Scouse Git"
12. "You Just May Be the One"
13. "For Pete's Sake"
14. "Pleasant Valley Sunday"
15. "What Am I Doing Hangin' 'Round"
16. "Words"
17. "Goin' Down"
18. "Daydream Believer"
19. "Valleri"
20. "D. W. Washburn"
21. "Porpoise Song (Theme from *Head*)"
22. "Listen to the Band"
23. "That Was Then, This Is Now"

24. "Anytime, Anyplace, Anywhere"
25. "Kicks"

(14) *The Monkees Live, 1967*
(Rhino Records / 1987)
1. "Last Train To Clarksville"
2. "You Just May Be the One"
3. "The Girl I Knew Somewhere"
4. "I Wanna Be Free"
5. "Sunny Girlfriend"
6. "Your Auntie Grizelda"
7. "Forget That Girl"
8. "Sweet Young Thing"
9. "Mary, Mary"
10. "Cripple Creek"
11. "You Can't Judge a Book by Looking at the Cover"
12. "I'm A Believer"
13. "Randy Scouse Git"
14. "(I'm Not Your) Steppin' Stone"

(15) *Missing Links, Volume One*
(Rhino Records / 1988)
1. "Apples, Peaches, Bananas and Pears"
2. "If You Have the Time"
3. "I Don't Think You Know Me"
4. "Party"
5. "Carlisle Wheeling"
6. "Storybook of You"
7. "Rosemarie"
8. "My Share of the Sidewalk"
9. "All of Your Toys"
10. "Nine Times Blue"
11. "So Goes Love"
12. "Teeny Tiny Gnome"
13. "Of You"
14. "War Games"
15. "Lady's Baby"
16. "Time and Time Again"

(16) *Missing Links, Volume Two*
(Rhino Records / 1990)
1. "All the King's Horses"
2. "Valleri"
3. "St. Matthew"
4. "Words"
5. "Some of Shelly's Blues"
6. "I Wanna Be Free"
7. "If I Ever Get to Saginaw Again"
8. "Come on In"
9. "I'll Be Back up on My Feet"
10. "Michigan Blackhawk"
11. "Hold on Girl"
12. "The Crippled Lion"
13. "Changes"
14. "Mr. Webster"
15. "You Just May Be the One"
16. "Do Not Ask for Love"
17. "Circle Sky"
18. "Cigars Theme"
19. "Riu Chiu"

(17) *Missing Links, Volume Three*
(Rhino Records / 1996)
1. "(Theme from) *The Monkees*"
2. "Kellogg's Jingle"
3. "We'll Be Right Back in a Minute"
4. "Through the Looking Glass" Previously Unreleased / Alternate Version
5. "Propinquity (I've Just Begun to Care)"
6. "Penny Music"
7. "Tear the Top Right off My Head"
8. "Little Red Rider"
9. "You're So Good"
10. "Look Down"
11. "Hollywood"
12. "Midnight Train" Demo Version

13. "She Hangs Out" Single Version
14. "Shake 'Em Up"
15. "Circle Sky" Alternate Mix
16. "Steam Engine" Previously Unreleased Alternate Mix
17. "Love to Love" Previously Unreleased Alternate Mix
18. "She'll Be There"
19. "How Insensitive"
20. "Merry Go Round"
21. "Angel Band"
22. "Zor and Zam" TV Version
23. "We'll Be Right Back in a Minute, No. 2"
24. "Tema *Dei Monkees*" (*The Monkees* Theme in Italian)

(18) *The Monkees Greatest Hits*
(Rhino Records / 1995)

1. "I Wanna Be Free"
2. "Mary, Mary"
3. "Randy Scouse Git"
4. "Goin' Down"
5. "D.W. Washburn"
6. "It's Nice to Be with You"
7. "(Theme From) *The Monkees*"
8. "Last Train to Clarksville"
9. "I'm A Believer"
10. "(I'm Not Your) Steppin' Stone" / Single Version
11. "A Little Bit Me, A Little Bit You"
12. "The Girl I Knew Somewhere"
13. "Pleasant Valley Sunday" Single Version
14. "Words"
15. "Daydream Believer"
16. "Valleri "
17. "Porpoise Song (Theme from *Head*)" Single Version
18. "Listen to the Band" Single Version
19. "That Was Then, This Is Now" Micky Dolenz & Peter Tork of The Monkees
20. "Heart and Soul"

(19) *Justus*
(Rhino Records / 1996)

    1. "Circle Sky"
    2. "Never Enough"
    3. "Oh What a Night"
    4. "You and I"
    5. "Unlucky Stars"
    6. "Admiral Mike"
    7. "Dyin' of a Broken Heart"
    8. "Regional Girl"
    9. "Run Away from Life"
   10. "I Believe You"
   11. "It's My Life"
   12. "It's Not Too Late"

(20) *The Monkees Anthology*
(Rhino Records / 1998)
Disc One

    1. "(Theme From) *The Monkees*"
    2. "Last Train To Clarksville"
    3. "Take A Giant Step"
    4. "I Wanna Be Free"
    5. "Papa Gene's Blues"
    6. "Saturday's Child"
    7. "Sweet Young Thing"
    8. "I'm A Believer"
    9. "(I'm Not Your) Steppin' Stone" Single Version
   10. "She"
   11. "Mary, Mary"
   12. "Your Auntie Grizelda"
   13. "Sometime In The Morning"
   14. "Look Out Here Comes Tomorrow"
   15. "I'll Be Back up on My Feet" TV Version
   16. "A Little Bit Me, A Little Bit You"
   17. "All of Your Toys"
   18. "The Girl I Knew Somewhere"

19. "You Told Me"
20. "Forget That Girl"
21. "You Just May Be the One"
22. "Shades Of Gray"
23. "For Pete's Sake"
24. "Randy Scouse Git"
25. "No Time"

Disc Two

1. "Pleasant Valley Sunday" Single Version
2. "Words" Single Version
3. "Daydream Believer"
4. "Goin' Down"
5. "The Door into Summer"
6. "Cuddly Toy"
7. "Love Is Only Sleeping"
8. "What Am I Doing Hangin' 'Round?"
9. "Star Collector"
10. "Valleri"
11. "Auntie's Municipal Court"
12. "Zor And Zam"
13. "Porpoise Song (Theme from *Head*)" Single Version
14. "As We Go Along"
15. "Circle Sky" Live Version
16. "Through the Looking Glass"
17. "You and I"
18. "While I Cry"
19. "Listen to the Band" Single Version
20. "Good Clean Fun"
21. "Mommy and Daddy"
22. "Oh My My"
23. "That Was Then, This Is Now" Micky Dolenz & Peter Tork (of The Monkees)
24. "Heart & Soul"
25. "You and I"

(21) *Music Box*
(Rhino Records / 2001)
Disc One

1. "(Theme from) *The Monkees*"
2. "I Wanna Be Free" Fast Version
3. "Let's Dance On"
4. "Last Train to Clarksville"
5. "Take a Giant Step"
6. "All the King's Horses"
7. "Saturday's Child"
8. "Papa Gene's Blues"
9. "I Wanna Be Free"
10. "Sweet Young Thing"
11. "Gonna Buy Me a Dog"
12. "I Don't Think You Know Me" First Recorded Version
13. "I'm a Believer"
14. "(I'm Not Your) Steppin' Stone"
15. "She"
16. "Mary, Mary"
17. "Your Auntie Grizelda"
18. "Look Out (Here Comes Tomorrow)" Previously Unissued Extended Version
19. "Of You" Previously Unissued Mix
20. "Look Out (Here Comes Tomorrow)" Previously Unissued Extended Version
21. "Sometime in the Morning"
22. "When Love Comes Knockin' (At Your Door)"
23. "Do Not Ask for Love" First Recorded Version
24. "Valleri" First Recorded Version
25. "I'll Be Back on My Feet Again"

Disc Two

1. "A Little Bit Me, A Little Bit You"
2. "She Hangs Out" Single Version
3. "The Girl I Knew Somewhere"
4. "All of Your Toys"

5. "Love to Love"
6. "You Told Me"
7. "I'll Spend My Life With You"
8. "Forget That Girl"
9. "You Just May Be the One"
10. "Shades of Gray"
11. "For Pete's Sake"
12. "Sunny Girlfriend"
13. "No Time"
14. "Randy Scouse Git"
15. "Pleasant Valley Sunday" Single Version
16. "Words"
17. "Daydream Believer"
18. "Goin' Down"
19. "Salesman"
20. "Door into Summer"
21. "Love Is Only Sleeping"
22. "Cuddly Toy"
23. "What Am I Doing Hangin' 'Round?"
24. "Daily Nightly"
25. "Star Collector"

Disc Three
1. "Valleri"
2. "Tapioca Tundra"
3. "Dream World"
4. "Auntie's Municipal Court"
5. "P.O. Box 9847"
6. "Zor and Zam"
7. "Carlisle Wheeling" First Recorded Version
8. "Tear the Top Right off My Head"
9. "Girl I Left behind Me" First Recorded Version
10. "Nine Times Blue"
11. "Come on In"
12. "D.W. Washburn"
13. "It's Nice to Be with You"
14. "St. Matthew"

15. "Porpoise Song (Theme from *Head*)"
16. "As We Go Along"
17. "Ditty Diego War Chant"
18. "Circle Sky" Live
19. "Can You Dig It?"
20. "Daddy's Song"
21. "Long Title: Do I Have to Do This All over Again"

Disc Four

1. "Tear Drop City"
2. "Man Without a Dream"
3. "Through the Looking Glass"
4. "I Won't Be the Same without Her"
5. "You and I"
6. "While I Cry"
7. "Shorty Blackwell"
8. "If I Ever Get to Saginaw Again"
9. "Smile"
10. "Listen to the Band" Single Version
11. "Someday Man"
12. "Some of Shelly's Blues"
13. "Mommy and Daddy"
14. "Good Clean Fun"
15. "Looking for the Good Times"
16. "Steam Engine"
17. "I Never Thought It Peculiar"
18. "Midnight Train"
19. "Oh My My"
20. "I Love You Better"
21. "Do You Feel It Too?"
22. "Do It in the Name of Love"
23. "That Was Then, This Is Now"
24. "Heart and Soul"
25. "MGBGT" Live
26. "Every Step of the Way" Single Version
27. "Oh What a Night"
28. "You and I"

(22) *The Essentials: The Monkees*
(Rhino Records / 2002)
1. "(Theme from) *The Monkees*"
2. "Last Train To Clarksville"
3. "I Wanna Be Free"
4. "I'm a Believer"
5. "(I'm Not Your) Steppin' Stone"
6. "A Little Bit Me, A Little Bit You"
7. "Pleasant Valley Sunday"
8. "Words"
9. "Daydream Believer"
10. "Valleri"
11. "Porpoise Song (Theme from *Head*)"
12. "For Pete's Sake"

(23) *Live Summer Tour*
Win Media Corp. / 2003
1. "Intro"/"Last Train to Clarksville"
2. "Valleri"
3. "Randy Scouse Git"
4. "Mary, Mary"
5. "Girl"
6. "Can You Dig It?"
7. "Goin' Down"
8. "Daydream Believer"
9. "I'm a Believer"
10. "(I'm Not Your) Steppin' Stone"
11. "For Pete's Sake"
12. "That Was Then, This Is Now"
13. "Porpoise Song (Theme from *Head*)"
14. "It's Nice To Be with You"
15. "Pleasant Valley Sunday"

(24) *The Best of The Monkees*
(Rhino Records / 2003)
1. "(Theme from) *The Monkees*"
2. "Last Train to Clarksville"

3. "I Wanna Be Free"
4. "Papa Gene's Blues"
5. "I'm A Believer"
6. "(I'm Not Your) Steppin' Stone"
7. "She"
8. "Mary, Mary"
9. "Your Auntie Grizelda"
10. "Look Out (Here Comes Tomorrow)"
11. "Sometime In The Morning"
12. "A Little Bit Me, A Little Bit You"
13. "The Girl I Knew Somewhere"
14. "Shades of Gray"
15. "Randy Scouse Git"
16. "For Pete's Sake"
17. "You Just May Be the One"
18. "Pleasant Valley Sunday"
19. "Words"
20. "Daydream Believer"
21. "Goin' Down"
22. "What Am I Doing Hangin' 'Round?"
23. "Valleri"
24. "Porpoise Song (Theme from *Head*)" Single Version
25. "Listen To The Band" Single Version

Karaoke Cuts
1. "(Theme From) The Monkees" Karaoke Version
2. "I'm A Believer" Karaoke Version
3. "(I'm Not Your) Steppin' Stone" Karaoke Version
4. "Pleasant Valley Sunday" Karaoke Version
5. "Daydream Believer" Karaoke Version

with Dolenz, Jones, Boyce & Hart

(1) *Dolenz, Jones, Boyce & Hart*
(Capitol Records / 1976)
1. "Right Now"
2. "I Love You (and I'm Glad I Said It)"
3. "You and I"

4. "Teenager in Love"
5. "Sail on Sailor"
6. "I Always Love You the Most in the Morning"
7. "Moonfire"
8. "You Didn't Feel This Way Last Night (Don't You Remember)"
9. "Along Came Jones"
10. "Savin' My Love For You"
11. "I Remember the Feeling"
12. "Sweet Heart Attack"

(2) *Dolenz, Jones, Boyce & Hart, Concert in Japan*
(Varese Records / 1996)
1. "Last Train to Clarksville"
2. Medley: "Valleri" / "Daydream Believer" / "A Little Bit Me, A Little Bit You"
3. "I Wonder What She's Doing Tonight?"
4. "(I'm Not Your) Steppin' Stone"
5. "I Wanna Be Free"
6. "Savin' My Love for You"
7. "Pleasant Valley Sunday"
8. "I Remember the Feeling"
9. "Teenager in Love"
10. "Cuddly Toy"
11. Medley: "Come a Little Bit Closer" / "Pretty Little Angel Eyes" / "Hurt So Bad"
12. "I Love You (And I'm Glad That I Said It)"
13. "Action"

Micky Dolenz Solo

(1) *Micky Dolenz Puts You to Sleep*
(Kid Rhino Records / 1991)
1. "Pillow Time"
2. "Dream a Little Dream"
3. "Beautiful Boy"
4. "Blackbird"
5. "Lullaby to Tim"

6. "Look on the Hill"
7. "Good Night"
8. "St. Judy's Comet"
9. "The Moonbeam Song"
10. "Remember"
11. "Sugar Mountain"
12. "The Porpoise Song"

(2) *Broadway Micky*
(Kid Rhino Records / 1994)
1. "Supercalifragilisticexpialidocious"
2. "Talk to the Animals"
3. "Somewhere Out There"
4. "Put on a Happy Face"
5. "You're Never Fully Dressed without a Smile"
6. "Never Ending Story"
7. "My Favorite Things"
8. "Ease on Down the Road"
9. "I Whistle a Happy Tune"
10. "Chim Chim Cheree"
11. "Me and My Arrow"
12. "When You Wish upon a Star"

Singles

*Certified Gold for sales in excess of one million copies
NOTE: Chart figures are according to Billboard Magazine from the American charts, unless otherwise noted

with The Monkees

1. "The Last Train to Clarksville" (1966) [Number One chart hit]*
2. "I'm a Believer" (1966) [Number One]*
3. "(I'm Not Your) Steppin' Stone" (1966) [Number 20]
4. "A Little Bit Me, A Little Bit You" (1967) [Number Two]*
5. "The Girl I Knew Somewhere" (1967) [Number 39]

6. "Alternate Title (Randy Scouse Git)" (1967) [Number Two / England]
7. "Pleasant Valley Sunday" (1967) [Number Three]*
8. "Words" (1967) [Number 11]
9. "Daydream Believer" (1967) [Number One]*
10. "Valleri" (1968) [Number Three]*
11. "Tapioca Tundra" (1968) [Number 34]
12. "D. W. Washburn" (1968) [Number 19]
13. "It's Nice to be with You" (1968) [Number 51]
14. "Porpoise Song (Theme from *Head*)" (1968) [Number 62]
15. "Tear Drop City" (1969) [Number 56]
16. "Listen to the Band" (1969) [Number 63]
17. "Someday Man" (1969) [Number 61]
18. "Good Clean Fun" (1969) [Number 82]
19. "Oh My My" (1970) [Number 98]
20. "Do It in the Name of Love" (1971)
21. "That Was Then, This is Now" (1986) [Number 20]

with Dolenz, Jones, Boyce & Hart

1. "I Remember the Feeling" (1975)
2. "I Love You" (1976)

Micky Dolenz Solo

1. "Huff Puff" (1966)
2. "Don't Do It" (1967) [Number 75]
3. "Easy on You" (1971)
4. "A Lover's Prayer" (1972)
5. "Daybreak" (1973)
6. "Buddy Holly Tribute" (1974)
7. "Lovelight" (1979)

Monkees on DVD

(1) *Our Favorite Episodes*
(Rhino / 2000)

(2) *Head*
(Rhino / 2000)

(3) *Live Summer Tour*
(Geneon Entertainment / 2003)

(4) *The Monkees / The Complete First Season*
(Rhino / 2003)

(5) *The Monkees / The Complete Second Season*
(Rhino / 2003)